THE REAL READER'S QUA...

Slightly Foxed

'Tarka the Rotter'

NO.35 AUTUMN 2012

Editors Gail Pirkis and Hazel Wood
Marketing and publicity Stephanie Allen and Jennie Paterson
Subscriptions Alarys Gibson and Anna Kirk

Cover illustration: Francis Hamel, *Magpie Lane with Tree*

Francis Hamel lives at Rousham in Oxfordshire with his wife and two teenage children.
He is represented by John Martin of London (38 Albemarle Street, London W1) where he will
show his second collection of Oxford paintings in December 2012. He also exhibits with the
Edward Cutler Gallery in Milan and with Marc de Puechredon in Zurich. For more details see
www.francishamel.com and www.jmlondon.com.

Cover fox: James Nunn, 'Donnish Fox'

Design by Octavius Murray

Layout by Andrew Evans

Colophon and tailpiece by David Eccles

Published by Slightly Foxed Limited
67 Dickinson Court
15 Brewhouse Yard
London EC1V 4JX

tel 020 7549 2121/2111
fax 0870 1991245
e-mail all@foxedquarterly.com
www.foxedquarterly.com

Slightly Foxed is published quarterly in early March, June, September and December
Annual subscription rates (4 issues)
UK £36; Europe £44; Rest of the World £48
Concessions are available for those aged 26 or under: please call the office
Single copies of this issue can be bought for £9 (UK), £11 (Europe) or £12 (Rest of the World)
Back issues are also available

ISBN 978-1-906562-41-0
Printed and bound by Smith Settle, Yeadon, West Yorkshire

Contents

Contents

Miriam Macgregor, 'Digging'

From the Editors

One of the most enjoyable things we do at *Slightly Foxed* – and there are many – is the commissioning of our covers. People often say they wish they could have reproductions of them, and so, in the spring, Alarys did some research, and we went off to visit a couple of small, environmentally friendly firms. One, in Lincolnshire, has now produced a lovely *Slightly Foxed* tea towel for us in hard-wearing unbleached cotton decorated with one of our most cheerful spring covers, and the other, in Berkshire, a mixed pack of four fine-quality cards of the most popular ones – two with a spring and summer and two with a winter theme.

We do hope you'll like these additions to our modest 'merchandizing' programme, and that they'll come in handy when Christmas arrives. Likewise the two latest in our series of little *Slightly Foxed* Paperbacks – Rosemary Sutcliff's *Blue Remembered Hills*, her vivid and unself-pitying account of how she grew up with a disability to become one of our best-loved children's writers; and *Corduroy*, Adrian Bell's classic picture of his life as a town boy working on a Suffolk farm between the wars.

We've embarked on another new experiment too this autumn – a Children's Catalogue. As time goes by it can be hard, when giving presents or choosing books for the children in our lives, to know who the good new authors are, and which of the books we once loved are still available. If you've signed up for our adult catalogue, you will automatically receive this one. But if you haven't and would like to receive either of them, do let us know. And do get in touch, too, if you're interested in attending our second *Slightly Foxed* Reader's Day in London on Saturday, 10 November, as we still have a handful of tickets left.

This season's new Slightly Foxed Edition is Alan Moorehead's *A Late Education* (see p. 13). Author of such bestselling books as *The White Nile* and *Gallipoli*, Moorehead was the perfect figure of the romantic writer and traveller, and a distinguished war correspondent in the Second World War. These vivid and haunting 'Episodes in a Life' describe his childhood in Melbourne, his apprenticeship as a journalist when he first arrived in Europe from Australia, and how, covering the war in the desert, he formed a close friendship with another young war correspondent, Alex Clifford, which lasted till Alex's premature death.

And finally, the difficult bit. We've been sitting round the table recently, drinking a lot of coffee and talking about money. Over the past few years we've valiantly held down the price of *SF* through three rises in postal charges, but the most recent one feels like the proverbial last straw. Any price increase will be modest, but we thought we should warn you that we're thinking about one. Meantime, we do so appreciate your loyalty, and hope that whatever happens you'll still feel that the pleasure you get from *Slightly Foxed* is cheap at the price.

GAIL PIRKIS
HAZEL WOOD

Our bookshop can obtain any of the books mentioned in this issue.
Slightly Foxed on Gloucester Road, 123 Gloucester Road,
London sw7 4TE, e-mail: enquiries@foxedbooks.com, tel: 020 7370 3503

Tarka the Rotter

JONATHAN LAW

If we're honest, most of us have at least one friend who we would hesitate to bring into civilized company – someone too strange or socially awkward, full of crazed notions about God or politics, given to boring on or making horrible scenes: unspeakable when drunk. Something similar holds with writers: there are books and authors that we love quite unreasonably but would hesitate to introduce to anyone nice. Often, these are the authors we read and read again, however many times we've given them up in despair or disgust, promising ourselves that we won't soil another moment in their company. As with many a difficult friendship, you can end up wondering who is abusing whom. Some knotty thoughts arise: doesn't allowing ourselves to feel ashamed of someone, anyone, always make us feel a bit ashamed of ourselves? Doesn't it imply a priggishness – at worst a kind of treachery?

The bothersome chap who prompts these thoughts is Henry Williamson – author of *Tarka the Otter* (1927), some lesser-known but exquisitely written animal stories, and twenty or so full-length novels, now largely unread except by a small band of cultists. Williamson seems a man made for mixed feelings: a naturalist of rare gifts, a writer with a unique voice and vision, but unquestionably a bore, a crank and – here it gets critical – an overt, unapologetic Nazi. His friends seem to have found him exasperating but lovable – a strangely feral, childlike creature: others saw something very dark and

Henry Williamson, *Tarka the Otter* (1927)
Penguin · Pb · 208pp · £8.99 · ISBN 9780141190358

had the perfect ready-made nickname for him: Tarka the Rotter.

There's a queasy fascination in seeing how this gifted, rather gentle man ended up where he did, a literary pariah still babbling shamelessly about Hitler as a 'chaste saint above earthly impulses' and a 'flawed Christ killed by the lack of imagination of others' in his novels of the 1960s; that, however, is a tale for another time. For the moment, I want to stay with the acceptable side of Williamson and to talk about his best-loved book; a book written almost a decade before he made his fateful visit to Germany and came away with the idea that Hitler – 'an ex-corporal with the truest eyes I have ever seen' – shared his own passion for ecology and agrarian reform. But even here, in *Tarka*, you might think you can see the portents – the little signs pointing to where it would all go so awfully wrong . . .

It's easy to feel attracted to the young Henry Williamson – the nerve-racked war veteran, still in his early twenties, who makes his way to North Devon on a battered motorbike, with a head full of Shelley and Richard Jefferies; who holes up in a tiny damp cottage – soon filled with cats, dogs, owls, gulls, a baby otter – and lives a hermit's or a tramp's life, exploring the wild country about him and starting to write it all down. This man we can agree to like, surely: he seems a bit like Snufkin, the unworldly drifter in the Moomin stories. He swims in the nude, he throws apples at local dignitaries, he scandalizes with his wild talk of Lenin and Christ.

Okay, so he's a bit worrying after all, this young man. But there's something inspiring, too, about the way he comes to write *Tarka* by a kind of deep immersion – plunging himself into the creature's habits and habitats, crawling through spinneys and splashing through rivers to get an otter's-eye view of the world. The tale has been frequently told, perhaps most eloquently by Robert Macfarlane:

Daily, for months, he walked out alone into the great wedge of moor that is held between the rivers Taw and Torridge, where they tumble, divergent, off the north-west slope of Dartmoor.

During those seasons of river haunting, Williamson lived through the moor's different weathers. Big scapular-shaped rain clouds, light trimming the wet rocks, coffee-coloured spate-water. At other times, sunlight, softness, wild swans beating through blue sky. Sometimes he slept out overnight, in the lee of a bank or in a stand of trees. He would wake starred with frost, or hung with dew. In the course of that strange and restless time, Williamson became, by his own reckoning, an otter-man.

In these early days, otter man took the same heroic trouble with his prose as he did with his fieldwork; *Tarka* was rewritten seventeen times, a few key chapters twice that. Williamson is, or can be, a virtuoso stylist:

> While the pallor of the day was fading off the snow a skein of great white birds, flying with arched wings and long stretched necks, appeared with a measured beat of pinions from the north. Hompa, hompa, hompa, high in the cold air . . . The beams of the lighthouse spread like the wings of a starfly above the level and sombre sands. Across the dark ridge of the Sharshook a crooked line of lamps winked below the hill.

That's a fairly randomly chosen piece from *Tarka*, but surely any Williamson fan would recognize it as his; when he's writing well, he has a wholly characteristic music – it's there in the 'measured beat' of the long, sonorous cadences, the repeated 'w', 'l', 'm' and 's' sounds (now I come to think of it, the sounds of his own name). It's a kind of incantation, and Williamson uses it to sing a whole world into being – a dreamlike world of starlit weir pools, precipitous, owl-hushed oak woods, grey plover-haunted estuaries, and high moors of cotton grass and curlew song. There's a glamour to these landscapes that is almost physically haunting.

So *Tarka* is justly a famous book and probably some kind of masterpiece. But ask precisely what kind and the questions begin to slide and wriggle and bite each others' tails. The book is as hard to get a hold on as its protagonist – and no more cuddly. The first thought to go has to be that this is in any way kids' stuff. Of all the strange books that have from time to time been thrust at children, *Tarka the Otter* must be one of the strangest. Shocking in its violence, heavy with descriptive detail, severely anti-anthropomorphic – it's a long way from *Watership Down*, let alone Disney. Any normal child would surely be bored and repelled (though the young Ted Hughes read it compulsively for two years: it 'entered me and gave shape and words to my world, as no book has ever done since').

But if it's not a children's tale, *Tarka* hardly conforms to the norms of adult fiction, either. Since the time of Jane Austen at least, our idea of the novel has been bound up with that of the self-aware, self-reflecting human consciousness – the sensitive individual looking before and after, questioning her own motives, growing through moral experience. And negotiating that other world, the social world of class and money, with all its tricky nuances. By contrast, Tarka's world is all appetite and instinct, with no room for introspection or moral discovery. The life of a wild animal is literally one thing after another, and markedly un-nuanced. To find a parallel in fiction you'd have to go to opposite ends of the literary spectrum – to the pulpiest sort of action thriller or something all French and experimental by Robbe-Grillet.

To tell the truth, it's not even one thing after another, this wild animal life – it's the same bloody thing, over and over and over. There's a short passage in *Tarka* that pretty well sums up the book:

[Tarka] caught a black and yellow eel-like fish, whose round sucker-mouth was fastened to the side of a trout . . . The sickly trout, which had been dying for days with the lamprey fastened to it, floated down the stream; it had been a cannibal trout and had eaten more than fifty times its own weight of smaller trout

. . . A rat ate the body the next day, and Old Nog [the heron] speared and swallowed the rat three nights later. The rat had lived a jolly and murderous life, and died before it could fear.

Agnes Miller Parker

Dog eat bird eat rat eat fish eat fish. this is Williamson's great theme and one that seems to inspire a keen ambivalence. Part of him, I suspect, thinks we should all just get on and lead a jolly murderous life, like his Nietzschean über-rat, while another part is wincingly aware of the pain in the world and yearns for some sort of Buddhist or Christian release. Everywhere in his work you'll find this divided sympathy, for the prey as for the predator. It comes out strongly and for many people uncomfortably whenever Williamson writes about hunting – he identifies with the terror of the hunted stag or otter, but also with the fierce glee of the hunter and with a mystical idea of life replenished through death. For Williamson, you feel, the hunt is less a form of pest control than the ritual expression of a cosmic principle – a code of death that can be read in the heavens as on earth:

By night the great stars flickered as with falcon wings, the watchful and glittering hosts of creation. The moon arose in its orbit, white and cold, awaiting through the ages the swoop of a new sun, the shock of starry talons to shatter the icicle spirit in a rain of fire. In the south strode Orion the Hunter, with Sirius the Dogstar baying green fire at his heels. At midnight Hunter and Hound were rushing bright in a glacial wind, hunting the false star dwarfs of burnt-out suns, who had turned back into Darkness again.

It's rather hard to know what to say about a passage like that – except that it's not exactly *Springwatch* ('Now over to Kate for the latest on those false star dwarfs . . .'). Though not always even a good writer, Williamson has the power to astonish that we normally associate only with the great artists. If you have the patience, and the stomach, you'll find passages of like power scattered throughout his works, even the mediocre or downright bad ones, not to mention those that are ideologically beyond anyone's pale. The question that most fascinates – and troubles – is how far Williamson's later views can be seen as a mad aberration, and how far they reflect toxins already latent in his thought. A 'religion of nature' can seem an attractive, life-affirming thing, but in practice it tends to go a bit like this: worship of nature shades into worship of vitality, which shades into worship of power, which shades into worship of cruelty. The *Tarka* world is one of pristine energies and a fierce purity of purpose that sits uneasily with the benign muddle of a democracy. Disconcertingly, it's the strong and radiant things in his work, as much as the weak and silly ones, that show how Williamson could be drawn to some form of fascism.

JONATHAN LAW is a writer and editor of reference books and a director of Market House Books Ltd. In The Dabbler (www.thedabbler.co.uk) Jonathan delves even deeper into the strange mind of Henry Williamson in some follow-up articles.

An Observer Observed

CHRISTIAN TYLER

The trouble with memoirs is that too often they are written by people whose idea of what's interesting is not the same as the reader's. They are either grossly self-serving, like most political memoirs, or a good story spoiled by bad writing. Autobiography is not easy: it calls for literary talent, professional detachment and moral courage.

Alan Moorehead had all three. Not only was he a rare example of a high-profile newspaper reporter who turned himself into a best-selling author, but he also had the vital extra ingredient of critical self-awareness. The result is an unusually good autobiography.

Fortunately for us, Moorehead had drafted *A Late Education: Episodes in a Life* before being incapacitated by a severe stroke at the age of 56 which left him unable to speak or write properly and reading only with difficulty. His wife Lucy Milner was also a journalist (they had met at the *Daily Express* where she was woman's editor) and she took on the job of editing her husband's draft for publication in 1970.

The heart of the book is the friendship between Moorehead and his fellow war correspondent Alex Clifford of the *Daily Mail*. Professional rivals and temperamental opposites, they first met in a bar in St Jean de Luz in 1938 and didn't hit it off. Meeting again in an Athens hotel in 1940, however, they found common ground and, having persuaded their respective newspapers to post them to Cairo, went through the rest of the Second World War together, from the Western desert, through Italy to Normandy and Paris.

The two were a perfect contrast. Alex was highbrow, diffident, well-educated, musically precocious and polyglot, but also indecisive, sexually shy and practically vegetarian. In describing his friend, Alan could see how very different he was himself: an energetic and ambitious young Australian, 'aggressive, erratic and full of enthusiasms', and in those days careless of others. Even physically they were opposites: Alan was small, Alex large.

Those who know Moorehead from *Gallipoli*, which launched his career as an author, or *The White Nile*, his most celebrated book, may be surprised by the character who emerges from *A Late Education*. A typical journalist, and the son of a journalist, he began his career on the *Melbourne Herald* but was desperate to get out of Australia. Bright rather than clever, energetic but not sporty, he was bottom of the class at school. His spelling was bad but his memory was good and he had – most importantly – a good 'nose'.

In those days journalism was a trade, not a profession, and it was not a fashionable career. Writing and spelling didn't count so much as curiosity about the world and a sceptical view of authority, with perhaps a touch of missionary zeal. It was a job which attracted misfits like Alan and Alex – misfits of a different kind – who preferred to watch the game of life from the touchline rather than join the scrum on the field. Journalists, in Moorehead's words, 'opt out of normal life because they choose to write about it'. Yet they live just as hard and quite often get killed for their pains.

Scenes from Moorehead's life are interspersed, but not in chronological order, with episodes describing the two friends at war. The latter are ironically titled 'To the Edgware Road', because Alex Clifford had a morbid notion that he would die in that shabby London shopping street which, says Moorehead, 'represented for him a way of life which he instinctively feared and loathed'.

Arriving in London in 1936, the young reporter found himself at last in a place where the news was not only being read but also made. A torrid affair with the exciting but unreliable 'Katherine' did not prevent him from setting off on his travels – and his late education. First he went as a freelance to Spain to look at the civil war, and was quickly thrown out. He dropped in to Berlin for the Olympic Games

and left a wonderfully mocking description of the Nazi fantasy con-
cocted around them. The road to the stadium was lined with 'statues
of the young demi-gods and goddesses . . . great bull-like young men
with truculent sexual parts and huge-bellied women carrying sheaves
of wheat'. The eyes of the girl he was chatting up on the street took
on a look of ecstasy when Hitler suddenly appeared through 'a forest
of outstretched arms'. And the Olympic village resembled nothing so
much as a stud farm where pampered young stallions with oiled skins
paraded around a compound, watched through the iron gates by
German girls with nostrils flaring like mares aroused.

The next year he was sent to Gibraltar, a 'hot and ugly little town',
from which he escaped by embarking on a mission to discover who
was sinking the ships running supplies from Turkey to the Spanish
Republican cities along the coast. In Istanbul he boarded the cargo
ship *Tinos*, carrying 8,000 tons of petrol, and after fighting off the
homosexual advances of the huge and drunken captain, survived to
witness a storm whose prelude he describes in words which Conrad
might have envied:

> I shivered on the bridge. All that concentrated heat from the
> iron decks had vanished, and the clean cold wind was rushing
> into every cranny of the ship, routing out the stale air and all
> the congested human smells we had brought from the Middle
> East. The sky was not yet entirely overcast. At several places
> where the flying clouds wore thin great rifts opened up, and
> looking through into the limpid cobalt space beyond we could
> see the new moon lying on its back, serene and yellow. For a
> minute or two it played a sickly light on the surface of the sea
> and the tossing bows of the *Tinos*, and then the clouds rushed
> across again, blotting it out with the rapidity and the com-
> pleteness of a camera shutter.

There followed an interlude in Paris, and the trip to St Jean de Luz
on the Spanish border where he first met Alex Clifford, and where he

saw the first column of Republican refugees coming over the Pyrenees.

The first year of the war in North Africa was the best time. Moorehead loved the desert because it reminded him of the Outback. (The cultured Alex much preferred Italy.) Desert war was confusing, however, like a game of chess on a board with no squares and no edges. But it was civilized: there were no civilians to be bombed or raped, no villages to be razed, no 'collateral damage'. Each day was the same. There was an hour of grace in the morning 'when the sky was filled with a cool apple-green light, but then the sun lifted its mad glaring eye over the horizon and the sense of dread returned'.

Fear of death affected the friends differently. Alan would go eagerly to the front but was afraid when he got there. Alex was jumpy on the way up, but appeared calm on arrival. On one of their many sorties, both very nearly lost their lives when their convoy drove into an Italian ambush in Cyrenaica.

For most soldiers, the shortage of amusements in the desert had an antiseptic effect so strong that even lust was tamed. Life was entirely directed towards a higher end, the defeat of the Nazi tyranny. Moorehead saw his existential problems suddenly resolved: the past was over, the whole world was in flux, and no one knew what the future held. For recreation, everyone went to Cairo, a comic city where camels carried hurricane lamps on their tails. It was the last-chance saloon. People plunged into a frenzy of dissipation, the men hypnotized by belly dancers in the nightclubs and the women gobbling cream cakes at Groppi's.

After the war, when Alex went on to greater things as a journalist, Alan gave up his job on the *Express* and retreated to Italy to become a writer. Here, living outside Florence, he enjoyed a further education. Improbably, he became the pupil and confidant of his neighbour, the elderly art historian Bernard Berenson. Tiny and frail, Berenson was strong-willed and had an encyclopaedic memory. He invited his new protégé to use the library at his villa, I Tatti, as a study. But he refused to talk about art.

Another cultural celebrity befriended in Italy was only too keen to discuss his work. Festooned with cartridge belts, carrying strings of dead teal and mallard round his neck, and with snow dusting his beard and woolly hat, Ernest Hemingway first appeared as 'the walking myth of himself'. The two men sat together for several days, talking of nothing but books and writing. Hemingway contradicted his public image, however: he was lonely, shy of publicity, and in the throes of writer's block.

A Late Education ends with the premature death of Alex from cancer in 1952, after the two friends had taken a final, wild and joyous ski run down the mountain at Kitzbühel. Clifford did not die in the Edgware Road, as he had feared. But he did lie there: it was where they took his body, to the mortuary.

Why are these memoirs so satisfying? Not because they describe great events or great personages, but because they are so expertly done. This is not the 'colour' writing of a well paid hack but real prose. The stories are not tailored for posterity to show their author in the best possible light; they appear to have been dashed off – albeit with the help of diaries – in the heat of the moment. Although they have been chosen to give us a flavour of the man, they are mainly about his times. Moorehead, for all his reputed pushiness, is unusually modest. Rarely does one find an observer so observant about himself.

CHRISTIAN TYLER is a former journalist. He worked for the *Financial Times* for 30 years.

Alan Moorehead's *A Late Education* (216pp), is now available from *Slightly Foxed* in a new limited and numbered cloth-bound pocket edition of 2,000 copies, each priced at £13.50 (plus p&p: UK £2.50, Europe £4.50, Rest of the World £5.50). Copies may be ordered by post (67 Dickinson Court, 15 Brewhouse Yard, London ECIV 4JX), by phone (020 7549 2121) or via our website www.foxedquarterly.com.

The following Slightly Foxed Editions are still available, at £13.50 each plus p&p:

Michael Wharton, *The Missing Will*
James Lees-Milne, *Another Self*
Ted Walker, *The High Path*
Graham Greene, *A Sort of Life*
Edward Ardizzone, *The Young Ardizzone*
P. Y. Betts, *People Who Say Goodbye*
Frances Wood, *Hand-grenade Practice in Peking*
Dodie Smith, *Look Back with Love*
Suzanne St Albans, *Mango and Mimosa*
Elspeth Huxley, *The Flame Trees of Thika*

The following titles are now available as Slightly Foxed Paperbacks, at £10 each plus p&p:

Adrian Bell, *Corduroy*
Ysenda Maxtone Graham, *Mr Tibbits's Catholic School*
Diana Holman-Hunt, *My Grandmothers and I*
Rosemary Sutcliff, *Blue Remembered Hills*

Not Swinging, Just Dancing

LINDA LEATHERBARROW

It was the early Sixties and I was 17. With only a small bag of clothes and some loose change, I ran away from home and caught the milk train to London. When the sky lightened and the rooftops crowded in, I leapt out on to an empty platform because the station had a friendly name – Seven Sisters. A week later, with my first wage, earned by selling toys in a department store, I bought myself a pair of black stockings, a bottle of frosted pink nail varnish, and a copy of Edna O'Brien's *The Country Girls*. My family believed books were 'good for you' and I'd gobbled up the classics: Dickens, the Brontës, Thackeray, Gaskell and Defoe, coping happily with long convoluted sentences and dutifully deploying them in my school essays. O'Brien's brilliantly concise sentences were a revelation, her voice fresh and direct.

Born in 1930 in Tuamgraney, County Clare, O'Brien was the only child of a fiercely Catholic family who believed the written word to be not only sinful but also sacrilegious. At school, she obsessively pored over the only books available – a huge dictionary and a tome on mycology; it wasn't until she arrived in Dublin that she discovered literature, reading James Joyce and the Europeans. In 1954 she eloped with the writer and divorcé Ernest Gébler, and moved to London where she fell in love with Fitzgerald and Hemingway and went to

Edna O'Brien, *The Country Girls* (1960) · 240pp · ISBN 9780752881164; *Girl with Green Eyes* (1962) · 256pp · ISBN 9780753821374; and *Girls in Their Married Bliss* (1964) · 176pp · ISBN 9780753821381, are all published in paperback by Phoenix, the first two at £7.99 and the third at £6.99.

work for Hutchinson as a publisher's reader. There, it soon became apparent that she had a special talent with words and, for £25, she was commissioned to write a novel.

The Country Girls, published in 1960, was both an attack on Ireland's insularity and an impassioned farewell. O'Brien's lyrical descriptions make it easy to imagine how homesick she might have felt, first in Dublin and then in post-war sooty London. Hedgerow flowers she remembers as 'little drizzles of blue and white and violet – little white songs spilling out of the earth'.

The novel's narrator, gauche and naïve schoolgirl Caithleen Brady, lives on a 400-acre farm where the big house has been burned down by the Black and Tans and everything is mud-splattered and 'going to ruin' or, like the rolled-up rugs, kept strict-ly for visitors. While Caithleen's mother struggles to hold farm and family together, her hapless father blows every penny on booze and gambling. 'Bills never worried Dada, he just put them behind plates and forgot.'

Mark Handley

Caithleen's father is frightening, but so is her best friend, witty and worldly-wise Baba Brennan, the vet's daughter. Baba, always on the make, uses strips of stolen sticking plaster from the surgery to draw attention to the round softness of her knees. She is both jealous of and unimpressed by Caithleen's infatuation with a much older mar-ried man, 'Mr Gentleman'. The latter, a Dublin solicitor, is French – hence his nickname (the locals can't pronounce his French one). With his weekends in the country, his impeccable manners and satin waistcoats, Mr Gentleman embodies romance and sensitivity – at least for Caithleen. But then the girls are lumped together at a convent boarding-school and locked into a world of sexual repression and bodily denial – rubber-soled nuns, cabbage-water soup – until Baba comes up with a scheme to get them both expelled, a scheme that involves delivering in writing 'the greatest shock of her religious life' to the Reverend Mother. Sent home in disgrace, they are packed off to Dublin to make a fresh start.

In Dublin, the girls share a room in a back-street boarding-house run by an indomitably aspirational German landlady, Joanna, who is 'one solid front of outstanding chest' and partial to home-made eggnog. Joanna's dialogue is a masterclass in the well-placed 'Mine Gott' as in 'Mine Gott Almighty save us!' on being asked for a second slice of cake. Caithleen finds work in a grocer's shop, Baba goes to college to take a course in Commerce, and Mr Gentleman shows up again, late one night.

Under the Censorship of Publications Act of 1929, the book was banned in Ireland, placing O'Brien in distinguished company. Books by Joyce, Hemingway, H. G. Wells, Daphne du Maurier, Emile Zola and even Barbara Cartland had also been banned, leading some opponents of censorship to re-name the Register of Prohibited Publications the 'Everyman's Guide to Modern Classics'. Being thought 'likely to corrupt and deprave' meant it was ten years before O'Brien's books became legally available in her own country.

Now, when sexually explicit scenes barely raise an eyebrow, it's hard to see why there was so much outrage. A young girl and an older man – Caithleen and Mr Gentleman – are alone together in the boarding-house sitting-room; they get undressed and look at each other, nothing more. Seeing his penis, Caithleen allows herself a sly little laugh: 'It was so ridiculous.' And perhaps that's why copies of the book were burned and O'Brien received hate letters. The stuff of melodrama, but O'Brien doesn't write melodrama. She deals in complex, subtle ways with the stuff of real life: loss, love, jealousy, laughter.

With my next wage packet, I rushed out and bought the sequel, *The Lonely Girl* (first published in 1962 and later reissued as *Girl with Green Eyes* in 1987). Again this is narrated by Caithleen, who now calls herself Kate. The girls are living in the same Dublin boarding-house, Kate is still working in the grocer's shop, and Baba is still at college, but the girls are more sophisticated now. They hire long dresses and silver shoes, smother themselves in perfume and pancake, and seek out the best bars and dance halls, where Baba finds men to pay for drinks and dinner.

Once more, Kate falls in love with an older, married man – Eugene Gaillard, a film-maker (documentaries on sewerage) – and, even worse in her family's eyes, a Protestant. But she is no longer a teenager; at 21 she may legally make her own choices. Nevertheless, when her father comes, mob-handed, to drag her away from Eugene's house, like a child she hides under the spare bed in the study. Listening to the men argue, she is amazed at her lover's coolly rational approach.

> He doesn't really want me, I thought as I took short, quick breaths and said an Act of Contrition, thinking that I was near my end. I don't know why I stayed under there; it was stifling.
>
> 'Would you turn?' my father said, and of course Eugene did not know what he meant by that.
>
> 'Turn?' he asked, in a puzzled voice.

Despite saying that she is pleased the Church no longer retains such a hold on Irish life, O'Brien remains a Catholic. 'There is a link between literature and spirituality. And to lose that would be to lose something very profound.'

In the final novel of the trilogy, *Girls in Their Married Bliss* (1964), the girls are living in London and this is another kind of novel altogether. If the first was Innocence, the second Experience, then this is Disillusion. Here the humour is bitter-sharp and, for the first time, the reader is given direct access to Baba's thoughts. Now the bored trophy-wife of a wealthy builder, she narrates the opening chapter with characteristic brio and toughness, describing her new husband as 'An Irishman; good at battles, sieges and massacres. Bad in bed.'

When the point of view moves back to Kate – also married – it is no longer in the first person, but the third, allowing the reader to feel Kate's increasing distance from her own actions. The powerful story swept me along and, as in the other two novels, O'Brien never insults the reader's intelligence, never explains. Kate struggles through a difficult separation from her husband and the small son she loves, but the resourceful Baba comes to the rescue, helping Kate find a bedsit and, finally, a house.

Living very much on the sidelines of Swinging London, with two small children of my own to look after, I found it all too easy to empathize with Kate. 'Come on, doll, you're not swinging,' complains a young man at a party.

> She would have liked to say, 'Teach me to dance,' or 'How many of these people sleep together?' but he was exercising his shoulders and flicking his fingers to the beat of the very loud music.
> 'You won't,' he said. 'You're not a primitive?'
> 'Later,' she said.

The trilogy is often described as autobiographical and, yes, O'Brien, like Caithleen, came from the west of Ireland, went to a convent school, and did work in a shop in Dublin (though a chemist's, not a grocer's). She also, like Kate, married an older man. However, for me, whether a story is true or imagined is neither here nor there. Much more important, and much harder to fabricate, is its emotional honesty. In O'Brien's novels this is never in doubt. Caithleen and Baba might not be 'swinging' in the well-worn Sixties sense, but O'Brien's prose never stops dancing. Light-footed and scrupulously true to life, the trilogy describes the drive towards independent fulfilment, the choices we all have to make – about sexual relationships, families, friendships – and the obligations that accompany those choices, and their sometimes savage rewards. Here it is, neither heroic nor condemnatory, but a fictional world that once really existed – that still does.

After four decades of city life, LINDA LEATHERBARROW is now a country girl again.

Considerable Indiscretions

DAVID SPILLER

The huge literature on Winston Churchill can seem impenetrable to the casual reader. Churchill's own writings, with their stentorian prose, do not always appeal (though *My Early Life* scores through its pell-mell pace of events). Martin Gilbert's official biography marshals the main themes superbly but cannot convey the everyday feel of Churchillian life. A host of Churchill's contemporaries have gone into print, reporting their dealings with the great man and basking in the light of his genius. Among them is Lady Violet Bonham-Carter, whose *Winston Churchill as I Knew Him* describes with beguiling insight her friend's life up to the year 1916. In the preface Bonham-Carter quotes Gray's remark to Horace Walpole: 'Any fool may write a most valuable book by chance, if he will only tell us what he heard and saw with veracity.' Such a man – though certainly no fool – was John (or Jock) Colville, one of the private secretaries to Churchill in both his spells as Prime Minister. During those periods Colville kept detailed diaries of events, which were published in 1985, two years before their author's death, as *The Fringes of Power: Downing Street Diaries, 1939–1955*.

When Churchill acceded to power in 1940, Colville was an impetuous young man of 25. To keep a written account in wartime, as he did, was to take one hell of a security risk. Even now one shudders at the thought of certain entries getting into the wrong hands ('The Cabinet are considering, very secretly, the possibility of bomb-

John Colville, *The Fringes of Power: Downing Street Diaries, 1939–1955* (1985), is out of print.

ing the Ruhr', *Nov. 1939*). Colville left the forbidden record locked in a drawer of his writing-table at 10 Downing Street; then, stricken by conscience, began moving it to his family home in Staffordshire, because 'its indiscretions were considerable'. Had he been rumbled it would have meant instant dismissal. He was amused to be told years later that the punishment for diary-keeping under Stalin's regime was death.

Seventy years on, posterity can only feel gratitude to the young Colville for taking such risks. And because, over the 800 pages of the published volume, he punctiliously eschewed making retrospective changes to the original entries, they now read like red-hot journalism rather than history. For in history – as Colville observed in 1944 – every event 'gains or loses colour and accuracy if described after the passage of time'.

Colville was a character. Martin Gilbert said so in his delightful book *In Search of Churchill*, highlighting the people who had helped with the official biography. Gilbert admitted to being 'somewhat afraid' of the then middle-aged martinet, always impeccably dressed, and with a low opinion – frequently expressed – of historians ('You people almost never get it right'). Though not wealthy, Colville was extraordinarily well-connected: a grandson of the Marquess of Crewe, and in his youth a confidant of Queen Mary. 'I do not think there was a single aristocratic family, however minor,' Gilbert wrote, 'that he did not know enough about to correct any conceivable error I might make.'

We learn a lot about the aristocratic lifestyle as the young Colville – in between his official duties – rides in Richmond Park, hunts, dances at the Savoy, plays croquet with Lady Churchill. And eats and drinks (in wartime!) with all the gusto of a man who was officially employed by the diplomatic service (oysters and champagne at Prunier's, *15 Nov. 1940*; sherry and smoked-salmon sandwiches at Diana Quilter's First Aid Post, *31 Mar. 1941*; even, 'lunched admirably' while flying over Casablanca, *14 Jan. 1944*).

Churchill's private staff, 1941:
Colville is to the left of Churchill

It was an era when ladies withdrew from the table after dinner and Colville, though susceptible to the opposite sex, could not take them seriously: 'It is a waste of time, and exasperating, to talk to most women on serious subjects.' Nevertheless he dined frequently with men *and* women, for here was someone who embraced networking before the term was invented. Whatever else readers skip in these diaries it should not be the footnotes which, appearing on almost every page, pithily sketch a roll-call of characters: Mrs Richard Norton, the 'deeply cherished friend and mistress of Lord Beaverbrook'; Lady Mary Glyn, 'a rather trenchant and occasionally quite interesting relic of another age'; Eddie Marsh, 'an aesthete with a prodigious memory [who] spoke in a high-pitched squeaky voice'.

Reading Colville, we discover the war all over again. We feel anxiety about an imminent invasion of Britain. We meet new characters ('There is apparently a young French General called de Gaulle'). We share the confusion and disbelief when a plane containing Rudolf Hess drops from the sky. The entries often relate great events to more personal details: 'As I dismounted the groom told me that Holland and Belgium had been invaded'; 'News that Paris has fallen. I am still reading *War and Peace*'; or, as Colville stays with relatives:

> During the afternoon an enemy raider surprisingly descended from the clouds and dropped eight bombs nearby – one hitting a train full of chocolate. Aunt Celia upset a silver kettle of scalding water over Lady Graham, but this was not cause and effect.

These are the diaries of a young man. 'There must be something wrong with me,' Colville writes in April 1940, for 'I just *cannot* take it tragically or feel nearly as depressed as I ought.' The following year we find him reading Pepys, and are struck by the similarities to his famous (and similarly youthful) predecessor: the curiosity, intelligent observation of events, turn of phrase, humour – and most of all the sheer enjoyment of life. As with Pepys, we forgive the diarist's little foibles and rejoice in his qualities.

For all those qualities, it is Churchill's personality that dominates the book. 'The P.M.'s absence makes an astonishing difference,' Colville notes in August 1941, and when the great man is missing from diary entries it is as if the blackout has extinguished all the lights of Downing Street. Fortunately Colville is usually Boswelling away by his leader's side – watching, listening, and then recording in a multitude of situations: Churchill with family, friends and colleagues; Churchill on the *Queen Mary*, or inspecting damage from the Blitz, or watching allied troops crossing the Rhine; Churchill walking and talking under the stars and demonstrating arms drill with his big game rifle; Churchill at mealtimes, dictating in bed, prostrate on the floor at Chartwell, or in his bath being briefed by Colville (with intermissions for submersions).

'When the women had gone to bed, I listened in the Great Hall to as interesting a discussion as I ever hope to hear,' Colville records, sitting in on meetings with the US envoy Harry Hopkins. Churchill 'talked of the past, the present and the future . . .' And we, his fortunate readers, can eavesdrop on everything that is said. Colville also has a knack of setting scenes visually:

> Went up to the P. M.'s bedroom at about 10.00 . . . He was lying in bed, in a red dressing-gown, smoking a cigar and dictating to Mrs Hill, who sat with a typewriter at the foot of the bed . . . His black cat Nelson . . . sprawled at the foot of the bed and every now and then Winston would gaze at it affectionately and say 'Cat, darling.'

At dinner, Churchill's conversation would mix state affairs with more playful topics:

> As a less serious epilogue, the P.M. discoursed on egalitarianism and the White Ant. He recommended Lord Halifax to read Maeterlinck. Socialism would make our society comparable to that of the White Ant. He also gave an interesting account of the love life of the duck-billed platypus.

It is especially intriguing to gaze over Colville's shoulder as Churchill prepares speeches and other communications. 'To watch him compose some telegram or minute for dictation is to make one feel that one is present at the birth of a child'; and 'Before dictating a sentence he always muttered it wheezingly under his breath and he seemed to gain intellectual stimulus from pushing in with his stomach the chairs standing around the Cabinet table.' Later on Colville observes: 'It is curious to see how . . . he fertilizes a phrase or a line of poetry for weeks and then gives birth to it in a speech'; then 'I followed the speech from a flimsy of the P. M.'s notes, which are typed in a way which Halifax says is like the printing of the psalms.'

Because the war's big events are already known, the accounts of Churchill's behaviour often fascinate more. That he was not easy to work for is a recurring motif. He was completely unpredictable, and inconsiderate with his staff's time. He would become hung-up on trivialities, as when he minuted the First Lord of the Admiralty urging the purchase of a new flag. His anger 'was like lightning and sometimes terrifying to see', though if it was unjust he 'seldom failed to make amends, not indeed by saying he was sorry but by praising the injured party generously for some entirely disassociated virtue'. Even so, the constant factor in relations with colleagues was the 'respect, admiration and affection that almost all those with whom he was in touch felt for him despite his engaging but sometimes infuriating idiosyncrasies'.

The second part of the diaries, covering Churchill's peacetime stint as Prime Minister (1951–5), is more spasmodic and less engaging than the first. Colville himself, no longer single, has lost some of youth's brio. ('Though marriage is an honourable estate, it is seldom a tonic for diarists unless they behave like Pepys.') And Churchill is more grievously affected by the passage of time, as his private secretary does not shrink from recording. 'On some days the old gleam would be there . . . the sparkle of genius could be seen in a decision, a letter or a phrase'; but 'he was reluctant to read any papers . . . or to give his mind to anything that he did not find diverting . . . more and more time was given to bezique and ever less to public business.' There is sadness but also an unmistakable sense of relief as the greatest living Englishman is eventually prised from office.

Rather than end on this doleful note, let us revisit Violet Bonham-Carter, recording her first meeting with the 32-year-old Churchill at a dinner in 1906, nine years before Colville was born. Churchill 'burst forth into an eloquent diatribe on the shortness of human life, the immensity of possible human accomplishments . . . in a torrent of magnificent language . . . and ended up with the words I shall always remember: "We are all worms. But I do believe that I am a glow-worm."' This remark presaged the events we are privileged to witness through John Colville's diaries.

DAVID SPILLER has twice kept diaries, which will never see the light of day.

The Black Isle and the Miss Boyds

VIVIEN CRIPPS

Reachfar is a ruin now. Approach, as we did, from the north, across rough, boulder-strewn fields, and it has a blind, sad look, just one small window in its long stone front. Go round to the other side and the mood changes. You are greeted by a blaze of gorse and a yard that has reverted riotously to moorland. Only a stone trough remains. But, for all its decay, the croft has a companionable air, although parlour, kitchen and attics are now all one and ivy pushes its way in over crumbling sills.

Reachfar, as it was in its bustling heyday, is the heart of Elizabeth Jane Cameron's first book, *My Friends the Miss Boyds*. I came across it when I was still at school, reading everything I could lay hands on as long as it wasn't one of my A-level set texts. For a Buckinghamshire girl who had never been further north than Rhyl, the portrayal of life in a remote, closely knit Highland community was bewitching, a glimpse of an unguessed-at world.

Narrated by 8-year-old Janet Sandison, the novel has immense vitality. An only child growing up at Reachfar in the First World War, Janet observes unfolding events with a wit and fierce intelligence inherited from her elders. When the local town of Achcraggan is invaded by a covey of Miss Boyds, a discordant note enters the even tenor of country life. Their desire to show how things are done in sophisticated circles in Inverness and their determination to catch a man – any man – provokes widespread amusement, masked by inscrutable Highland politeness. But, as the war ends, irresistible comedy gives way to an Ophelia-like tragedy. Though life returns to its normal rhythms and everyone but Janet seems to have forgotten

Miss Violet Boyd, profounder changes loom: economic depression will threaten the rural way of life in a way that the foolish Miss Boyds never did.

The book carries unshakeable conviction: this is a writer who knows her landscape and people intimately. Indeed, Cameron is drawing a map of the part of her childhood she loved best, her school holidays at her grandparents' croft, the Colony, her 'real home'. The croft, the countryside and the hard, satisfying, self-sufficient life provide the setting and dictate the pace of the story – just as the eccentricities of her family and friends colour it, and her own early fascination with words lends freshness to the telling.

The Colony stands high on the northern flank of the Black Isle. Despite its name, the Black Isle isn't an island at all but a peninsula just north of Inverness, between the Moray and Cromarty Firths. Tiny, attractive towns dot the coast, while behind them rises moorland. The area was known to relatively few until *My Friends the Miss Boyds* took the literary world by storm in 1959. Cameron had written it (and six other books) while living in Jamaica with her partner Sandy. She kept her writing secret, hiding the manuscripts in her linen cupboard and only seeking a publisher when Sandy became seriously ill. Publishing history was made when Macmillan accepted all seven. Back in the UK after Sandy's death, she became a reluctant overnight celebrity.

I'd wanted to visit the Black Isle ever since I first read the book but it was to be nearly forty years before I did so. In the late spring of 2008, two old university

Kate Baylay

friends, Christine, who is married to the author's nephew Neil, Kate, a writer, and I arranged a long weekend there. We were to stay in the cottage in Jemimaville that Cameron shared with her Uncle George when she returned from Jamaica. I was thrilled but apprehensive. The once best-selling *Miss Boyds* was long out of print and I wondered if the places it brought so triumphantly to life would still be there.

They were. We walked up to the Colony on our first morning, leaving the sparkling blue of the Cromarty Firth below us. A narrow path led us through dappled woodland and swathes of bluebells, past broken, mossy walls and a silent, reed-filled lake, until the way was barred by impenetrable thickets and we were forced to wriggle through barbed wire and negotiate ploughed fields to reach our goal.

Bypassing the byre and stepping inside the living quarters, we found remnants of mottled plaster clinging to the rough stones, deep slots where attic floor beams had rested, a battered frame askew in the small north window. Against one wall was the rusting kitchen range where poor, mad Miss Violet Boyd sat docilely while Grandmother and Lady Lydia admired her dead rabbit 'baby'.

Next, Christine drove us along the shore road to Cromarty, the real-life Achcraggan. Today the little town, with its plain, pleasing Georgian houses, bright gardens and short streets seeming to end in the sea must still look much as it did a hundred years ago. Any visiting *Miss Boyds* fans will, I promise, feel a surge of delighted recognition as they wander round. Here is the pier where the coal boat arrived once a year (a great event, for it always carried inte-resting extras along with the official cargo); here the maze of white-washed cottages in Fisher Town, where 'the brown-faced, sloe-eyed, barefoot' fish-seller Bella Beagle lived; here the sea wall where the six Miss Boyds sat giggling as a destroyer dashed in with news that the Great War was finally over; and here the long white inn where the child of shame 'Andra' Boyd made his reappearance as a fully fledged spiv in the 1940s. By some miracle, the early twentieth century *has* survived into the twenty-first.

Beside the sea, a sweep of close-cropped turf leads to a tall, gaunt stone, a memorial to those driven out by the Clearances – still fresh in sheep-hating Grandmother's folk-memory. On the hill above is the church where the black-bearded Reverend Roderick battled against his congregation's tendency to sin. Many Camerons are buried here but not Elizabeth Jane. To find her grave, you must return along the shore road to the inner curve of Udale Bay. Here, in a tranquil grave-yard by the ruins of Kirkmichael church, a simple headstone looking over the water to Jemimaville records the *nom de plume* by which readers all over the world knew her: Jane Duncan.

* * *

That evening, as we sat nursing glasses of wine by a log fire in Rose Cottage, Christine remembered her aunt-in-law's papers stacked in the cupboard under the stairs. Enthralled, we dragged the boxes through to the little sitting-room and began to delve. Brown-paper parcels tied up with string held typescripts of her published books; torn manila envelopes bulged with early, unpublished writing. A stack of business-like desk diaries were filled with brief, telling entries of her post-war life in Jamaica and Jemimaville; earlier fragments tucked into an exercise book gave tantalizing glimpses into her time in the WAAF. And fat scrapbooks, assiduously assembled by Uncle George, contained reviews of her books – an impressive reminder of the impact she made.

By the time she died in 1976, Jane Duncan had written more than thirty books, translated into several languages, and acquired an eager readership around the world. Besides the first seven *My Friends* titles accepted in a batch by Macmillan, she wrote a dozen more in the sequence. The novels mirror the progress of her own life, from secre-tary-companion in 1930s England (*My Friend Muriel*) to the WAAF and early married life (*My Friend Monica*), the gorgeous, alien en-vironment of the Caribbean (*My Friend Sandy* and others) and the return to the Black Isle. In all of them, autobiography and imagination are blended in a witty, acerbic, compassionate mix uniquely her own; in all of them Reachfar, whether physically present or not, is an underlying force, the enduring standard by which she measures the outside world.

The three of us read and drank and talked far into the night, astonished that a writer with such a distinctive voice had been allowed to fall out of print. We found her birth certificate. It was, we discovered, less than two years until her centenary. We resolved that something must be done.

In 2010, as part of the Jane Duncan centenary celebrations, VIVIEN CRIPPS's publishing house Millrace brought out a new edition of Jane Duncan's *My Friends the Miss Boyds* (1959) (Pb · 288pp · £12.50 · ISBN 9781902173313). Reviews and reactions that summer showed that her writing has not lost its appeal. In 2011 Millrace also reissued *My Friend Monica* (1960) (Pb · 272pp · £12.50 · ISBN 9781902173320).

An Epiphany at the British Museum

C. J. WRIGHT

Many young men feel trapped and unappreciated in uncongenial jobs, and on a hot summer day in 1871 one 22-year-old felt more frustrated than most.

Edmund Gosse, son of the famous naturalist Philip Henry Gosse, had worked at the British Museum since he was 17. His father's friend Charles Kingsley had helped secure him the post of Junior Assistant in the Department of Printed Books. For someone with literary ambitions, this must have seemed an attractive position but it was, in fact, a clerical treadmill. With the other Juniors, his task was simply to write out the seemingly endless stream of revised entries prepared by his seniors for the catalogue of what was then the largest library in the world.

The sense of imprisonment was made worse by his working conditions. The Junior Assistants were confined in the south-west basement of the iron book-stacks that encircled Panizzi's new Reading Room. Gosse later described it as 'a singularly horrible underground cage, made of steel bars, called the Den'. The bars were to allow light to filter in since there was no artificial lighting. It was freezing in winter and stifling in summer. A number of deaths were attributed to it. The resulting scandal even reached the pages of *The Times*.

On this particular day, however, in these hot and gloomy sur-

Edmund Gosse, *Father and Son* (1907)
OUP · Pb · 304pp · £8.99 · ISBN 9780199539116
Gosse's essay on Tennyson, 'A First Sight', appears in Edmund Gosse, *Portraits from Life*, ed. Ann Thwaite (Scolar Press, 1991), now out of print.

roundings heavy with the scent of rotting leather, Gosse's labours were interrupted. One of the Senior Assistants, who had been keeping a friendly eye on him, descended literally from on high and appeared at his desk.

William Ralston was an imposing, almost patriarchal figure – six feet six inches tall, with a beard that reached to his waist. Though destined to come to a sad end, at this stage he was still a rising star, a distinguished Slavonic scholar, the friend and translator of Turgenev. He was also on familiar terms with many famous authors. He brought the exciting news that there was an important visitor upstairs in the Museum, one of the towering literary figures of the day, Alfred Tennyson.

Ralston wanted to take Gosse upstairs and introduce him to the Poet Laureate. It was a singular honour but Ralston's confidence in Gosse was not misplaced. Over the course of a literary life extending almost another sixty years, Gosse was to meet and befriend a multitude of authors and to describe many of them in his writings. Indeed, such was the position he came to exercise in the literary world that H. G. Wells famously characterized him as 'the official British man of letters'.

Before describing Gosse's encounter with the author of *In Memoriam* and *The Idylls of the King*, it is worth reflecting on his later admission that the Victorians carried their admiration of individuals to too high a pitch: 'they turned it from a virtue into a religion, and called it Hero Worship'. To do this we must move forward half a century towards the end of Gosse's career. In 1918, he was to review one of the latest literary sensations of the age, Lytton Strachey's *Eminent Victorians* (see *SF* no. 33). He was well aware that this volume was but one manifestation of an intellectual revolution which had been rapidly gathering pace and which dismissed many aspects of Victorian art, literature and architecture as readily as 'the glued chairs and glass bowls of wax flowers of sixty years ago'. To much of this movement Gosse was decidedly sympathetic, not least in the sphere of biography. His particular *bête noir* was the two-volume 'Life and Letters', whose pompous platitudes commemorated in print the recent dead.

As it happens, a particularly egregious example of the form was the life of Tennyson himself written by the poet's son, and Gosse made merciless fun of its preening pieties.

> Thus the priesthood circled round their idol, waving their censers and shouting their hymns of praise, while their ample draperies effectively hid from the public eye the object which was really in the centre of their throng . . . Their fault lay not in their praise, which was much of it deserved, but in their deliberate attempt in the interests of what was Nice and Proper – gods of the Victorian Age – to conceal what any conventional person might think not quite becoming. There were to be no shadows in the picture, no stains or rugosities on the smooth bust of rosy wax.

Gosse spoke with feeling. Though he had himself produced an orthodox biography of his father, his most famous work, *Father and Son*, written at the prompting of George Moore, famously subverts the traditional form. The book is so well-known that it is easy to forget today how revolutionary this frank examination of his father's religious faith and its unhappy effect on his only child actually was. In short, Gosse was a pioneer of candid autobiography. He had also had an unhappy experience when writing one of his later biographies. He hinted at this when he observed in 1912: 'The great danger of twentieth-century biography is its unwillingness to accept any man's character save at the valuation of his most cautious relatives, and in consequence to reduce all figures to the same smooth forms and the same mediocre proportions.' As prophecy, this was to be wide of the mark, but it accurately sums up his own recent tribulations.

In his opinion, of all his friends the most remarkable had been Algernon Charles Swinburne, a writer he was convinced would take his place as 'one of the few unchallenged Immortals'. Gosse determined that he should portray him for posterity. Unfortunately, when Swinburne died his closest surviving relatives were two elderly ladies, his sister Isabella and his cousin and former sweetheart Mary Disney Leith. These stoutly maintained that Swinburne did not drink (he was an alcoholic), was a practising member of the Church of England (he was an atheist) and would never have spoken to a woman like the equestrian *artiste* Adah Isaacs Menken (she was briefly his mistress). So as not to cause them distress, Gosse felt bound to respect their wishes. The subject of flagellation was not even raised. For Gosse himself some forms of truth were unacceptable. However, these facts were widely known. In consequence, Gosse's biography was ill received.

With all this in mind we can now return to that hot summer day fifty years earlier when in Ralston's wake Gosse scurried up the spiral metal staircase from the Museum basement for his introduction to the literary colossus of the age.

Gosse described his meeting with Tennyson as taking place in 'the long First Sculpture Gallery'. This was, in fact, the gallery at the south of the Museum which runs west from the Front Hall towards the Assyrian and Egyptian Galleries. Latterly it has been given over to postcards and left luggage but at this period it was the Roman Gallery and we need to imagine it as it was in its prime. On one side, beneath the windows looking out on Smirke's Grecian colonnade, were Roman antiquities discovered in Britain; on the other Roman mosaics were affixed to the walls and beneath them were rows of statues and busts of Roman rulers from Julius Caesar to Gordian I. In the centre of the gallery stood the striking if heavily restored marble equestrian statue of a naked young Julio-Claudian prince, then thought to be Caligula.

There among the sculptures was Tennyson with his close friend James Spedding, the editor and biographer of Sir Francis Bacon. Looking back, Gosse clearly retained the sense of awe he felt on that day. 'Tennyson was scarcely a human being to us, he was the God

Daniel Macklin

of the Golden Bow.' In his mind's eye, Tennyson stood there among the Roman emperors as if he were one of them.

With exquisite tact, Ralston engaged Spedding in conversation so that Gosse could have the great poet to himself. Gosse's own first volume of poems had been published the year before. It had sold twelve copies. Tennyson seemed aware of it and was 'vaguely gracious' about Gosse's verse. Ralston had told Tennyson that Gosse was about to visit Norway. Tennyson described his own visit. The young man was totally overcome in the presence of his hero. He could scarcely utter a word.

What could have been an embarrassing silence was interrupted by someone suggesting that they look at the sculptures. In retrospect, what struck Gosse was how swarthy Tennyson was. He thought that his friend Hamo Thornycroft had caught the essence of him in the statue later erected at Trinity College, Cambridge, but only if the lightness of the stone were converted into dark.

This transposition may have influenced his memories of the occasion for he extended it from its subject to his surroundings. He described Tennyson stopping in front of 'the famous black bust of Antinous'. In fact, Hadrian's favourite, portrayed with the attributes of Bacchus and, in the words of a later curator, displaying 'a sullen and sensual expression', is fashioned out of white Parian marble. The Laureate remarked 'Ah! this is the inscrutable Bithynian,' before adding himself, equally inscrutably, 'If we knew what he knew, we should understand the ancient world.'

When Gosse came to describe this episode in his essay 'A First Sight', published in 1912, he did not disguise that what he felt for Tennyson was hero-worship, though he doubted if such a feeling were any longer possible: 'no person living now calls forth that kind of devotion'. The familiarity occasioned by cheap newspapers and abundant photographs had dispersed the aura of sanctity and romance that surrounded popular idols. He did not guess that precisely this proliferation of information would feed other forms of celebrity. He also did himself a serious injustice. His feelings, as he describes them, were far from ridiculous and he portrayed them with touching sensitivity, vividly recapturing the experiences of youth.

Gosse understood that the vital thing for any biographer is not to like or approve of their subject but to try to understand them. For this, you need 'sympathetic imagination'. It was a quality his own parents had lacked with such disastrous results for his childhood, and it was just such a lack, for all his admiration of his 'pellucid stream of prose', that he detected in Lytton Strachey. In consequence, Strachey's characters were not living people but amusing puppets. By contrast, what Gosse sought to convey in his pen portraits was reality. In this sense, he was more modern than Strachey. He was striving for a world in which representations of Tennyson and Antinous were neither white nor black, because people are more complicated than that and everyone, without exception, is a shade of grey.

C. J. WRIGHT was Keeper of Manuscripts at the British Library until his retirement in 2005.

The Art of Browsing

OLIVER PRITCHETT *on some more elementary do's and don'ts of book etiquette*

It is time to reclaim the verb 'to browse'. Its proper meaning is 'to linger in a bookshop, sampling the volumes on display'. These days the word is too often appropriated by Internet addicts and goats. When we sit at our keyboards and trawl through websites the correct verb should be 'to gawp'. And when goats, with their insolent expressions, tear at sparse vegetation in scrubland, they are simply chomping. Browsing in a bookshop is an art, and therefore involves certain rules, which I am now going to explain.

The first thing to remember is that, as a browser, you are part of the bookshop's ambience. You have a non-speaking, walk-on part in a great tableau. There are two possible poses to strike and I call these the Nonchalant and the Devotional. With the Nonchalant you put your weight on one leg and lean decoratively on, say, the Fiction A–Z section, resting your right elbow on the H shelf (e.g. Robert Harris to Joseph Heller) while holding the book in your left hand. When you adopt the Devotional pose, you don't lean and you hold the volume in front of your face with both hands, as if it were a hymn book.

You should never sit on the floor, having made an encampment with rucksack, coat, packet of Prêt à Manger sandwiches, Tesco shopping bags and a takeaway coffee cup. That makes the place look like a budget airline departure lounge. So remember the rule: only children may sit on bookshop floors.

Some distinctions need to be made here: first of all, browsing is not the same as lurking. Hanging about in the History section or loitering in Biography is just going to unsettle other customers. And browsing is not the same thing as riffling, which is frowned on, except in university bookshops where it is called revising for exams.

What is the browser's purpose? It may be to help him or her decide whether to buy the book or it may be an attempt to get the gist of the thing so that he or she can bluff in the company of cultivated acquaintances. The browser must, of course, show consideration towards the bookshop owner. It is rather like sampling a discreet grape or two in a supermarket; that may be tolerated, but a banana would be over-

Daniel Macklin

stepping the mark. So there are time limits to be observed. As a general rule, 1 hour and 10 minutes is the maximum browsing time for fiction, while it is 44 minutes for non-fiction. If you are heading for the exit without a book after spending the maximum browsing time in the shop, it is considered appropriate at least to buy a greetings card or, perhaps, an orange and white Penguin coffee mug.

Some people can get through a hefty novel by reading a chapter at a time, each in a different bookshop. This is the literary equivalent of a pub crawl, though if you happened to meet one of these persons in a pub you might be impressed by their erudition, but you can be sure they are not going to buy you a drink.

In the Reference section you may encounter the browser-on-the-run. This is the individual who has darted in to get urgent help with a crossword clue, to check something in the *Oxford Dictionary of Quotations* or a Swedish phrase-book, or to look up 'Downy mildew' in the index of a gardening book. There are also those people who come to find their symptoms in the medical encyclopaedias. Remember, if you do this, not to linger too long, as there may be other patients waiting to consult the book. (Some medical encyclopaedias, featuring the most interesting ailments, are wrapped in cellophane these days, which can be a severe blow to hypochondriac bibliophiles.)

Tim O'Kelly, the owner of the One Tree bookshop in Petersfield, tells me that occasionally people will take a big glossy cookery book from the shelves, then ask to borrow a pen so that they can copy out a recipe. This, I would say, is definitely Not Done, but Mr O'Kelly manages to grin and bear it. 'You have to play the long game,' he says philosophically.

These days, many bookshops use the smell of freshly brewed coffee to lure their customers in and to show us that the way to a Larkin is through a latte. This raises all sorts of questions about the etiquette of browsing in bookshop cafés. Is it ever acceptable to eat a doughnut while dipping into Katherine Mansfield? Can you be sure that Ian Rankin's skill at creating tension will not cause you to spill your Americano on page 49 of the Inspector Rebus mystery?

Mr O'Kelly, taking the long view in Petersfield, is, of course, relaxed about his customers taking volumes to the shop's café, and so are other shops. They are even tolerant in Waterstones, which has 80 cafés (some selling soup) in its 300 stores. They take the view that the benefits of café browsing outweigh any damage that may occur, and the longer people spend in their stores the better. Purist browsers will see all this as a sad decline in standards. It is, in some way, just a bit too convenient to be the done thing – like boil-in-the-bag rice, Velcro or pocket calculators. A little discomfort, after all, shows that you are totally absorbed in what you are reading.

Finally, there is just one more important thing to mention. If you are, at this very moment, in a bookshop reading *Slightly Foxed*, in either the Nonchalant or the Devotional manner, may I politely suggest that you take it to the till and purchase it without any further ado?

OLIVER PRITCHETT has previous convictions for loitering with intent by the shelves of the Crime section in a number of bookshops.

Living in Interesting Times

C. J. DRIVER

I don't suppose anyone really understands why some novelists, widely read, even celebrated, are eclipsed when they die. Why is R. C. Hutchinson (1907–75) now almost forgotten? *The Unforgotten Prisoner* (1933), his third novel and first success, sold 150,000 copies in the month of publication. *Rising*, his last novel, the final chapter unfinished when he died, was short-listed for the Booker Prize in 1975. It isn't that publishers haven't tried. Allison & Busby republished several of the novels as 'modern classics' in the 1980s and 1990s. *Testament* (1938) and *The Unforgotten Prisoner* were reissued as King Penguins in 1981 and 1983. And now Faber have reissued five of the novels as Faber Finds: *The Unforgotten Prisoner*, *Testament*, *Recollection of a Journey* (1952), *A Child Possessed* (1964) and *Rising*.

In fact, according to Hutchinson's bibliographer, Robert Green, his career was 'mysteriously inchoate': 'spurts of recognition would be followed by years of anonymity'. Rupert Hart-Davis, in his foreword to the bibliography (there appears to be no biography), thought Hutchinson's reclusiveness might be the reason: 'All his life, regardless of fashion, neglect or misunderstanding, he pursued his solitary way, taking no part in what is called literary life, attending no parties.' His 'solitary way' did include what one guesses was a happy marriage, but there are suggestions of long-term ill-health. Hutchinson himself thought his war-service didn't help: 'The gap of five and a half years

R. C. Hutchinson, *The Unforgotten Prisoner* (1933), *Testament* (1938), *Recollection of a Journey* (1952), *A Child Possessed* (1964) and *Rising* (1975) are all available in paperback as Faber Finds, at between £15 and £20 each.

in the very middle of my professional life was no more helpful to me than to people in other callings.'

There may be other reasons. None of the novels I have read is easy to read. They move very slowly – and in an 'apologia' published in 1949 Hutchinson insisted this was a necessity:

> The situations and events of a novel can derive importance only from the importance of the people who take part in them . . . the reader must know those people as he knows his own friends. In life such intimate knowledge is acquired as a rule slowly . . . Indeed, I suspect that slowness (the tedium of which ought to be cunningly alleviated) is an element essential to the novelistic form – as opposed to the dramatic or short-story form . . .

Hutchinson himself worked very slowly; and the realism of the novels is created by the accumulation of meticulous detail. They are not autobiographical: though the starting-point may have been some personal experience, creating the world of each novel involved what he called 'donkey work'. Asked how he had obtained the knowledge of Russia he needed for *Testament*, he wrote: 'The answer is grievously simple. Municipal libraries contain many books by amateur travellers, naïve autobiographers, excitable diarists and others, which are full of odd bits of information . . .' In our time, the difference between the novel and the memoir has been blurred, so the novelist who hasn't found things out from actual experience, but who merely makes them up, is thought in some way to be cheating.

Hutchinson's profound Christianity may also have repelled some readers. Hart-Davis says there is an 'underlying assumption, which permeates all Hutchinson's works, that Christian love is the only hope for the world'. Hutchinson himself disdained didactic purpose, but he also wrote: 'The splendour possible in fiction will never come, I think, except from discovering in every human (good or bad, intelligent or idiotic) a value far higher than that which he derives from having, in the last few hundred millennia, come to surpass the lower animals in sentience and understanding: an individual and unique value, acquired from an extra-natural source.'

Probably the best novel for a reader unacquainted with his work to start with is *A Child Possessed*, regarded by Hart-Davis as 'the apogee of his creative genius'. Not only is it shorter than most of the other major novels but the cast of characters is manageable, and the moral passion impossible to gainsay. An exiled Russian aristocrat turned lorry-driver takes his severely handicapped daughter out of the home to which she has been confined so that she won't have to have the brain surgery that might make her more manageable, and then cares for her while travelling in southern France. In the process, his relationship with the child's mother, an actress who deserted him and the child to resume her career, is resuscitated. It is an extraordinary book, beautifully crafted and deeply moving.

Yet, though I love and admire that novel, I think in the end Hutchinson's greatest works are those which look at the broad sweep of European history, in particular *Recollection of a Journey*, about the plight of refugees in post-war Europe, *March the Ninth* (1957), about the aftermath of a Nazi atrocity, and *Johanna at Daybreak* (1969), covering some of those same themes, and which Robert Green calls 'a towering commentary on modern European history that will one day be properly assessed as a classic of our time'. All deserve essays of their own; but here I want to concentrate briefly on an earlier novel, *Testament*, set in Russia during the Bolshevik Revolution.

A prefatory note by 'R.C.H.' purports to explain that his book is based on a faithful adaptation, although with names changed, of a memoir given him in Paris by Captain Alexei Otraveskov, and mainly about his friendship with Count Anton Scheffler, executed in Moscow by the Communists as a counter-revolutionary, although he had for years been regarded as a resolute ally of the proletariat.

It is a huge novel, and the list of the more important characters runs to fifty-one names. Some, such as Prince Roumaniev and his wife Tatiana Vascovna, are aristocrats. Others belong to the professional classes: Dr Mishlayevski looks after Ivan, the Otraveskovs' crippled son, while the Jewish lawyer Strubensohn tries valiantly to get Scheffler released from prison. Then there are the committed Communists – Otraveskov's sister, for example, who is terrifying in her certainty of rectitude – as well as the crooks and time-servers and servants.

This is a work of the imagination, not of history. However, the accuracy of his depiction of the effects of solitary confinement (of which I have a little experience) is undeniable. Similarly the effect of sleep deprivation (of which, mercifully, I have no experience) is described with a dramatic vividness unsurpassed by anything else I have read. The interrogators want Otraveskov to confess that he knew Scheffler was a Tsarist agent and that his support of the revolution was merely a pretence. The lights in the cell are never put out. The guard keeps waking him. An agent provocateur is put into the cell and talks and talks and talks, pretending to implicate Scheffler.

Three nights – or was it four nights? – that went on. Sometimes he let me drop asleep, only to wake me a few minutes later. Sometimes I struck out at his face, but it was easy for him to dodge that, and by way of reward he would hold my ears and shake my head rhythmically from side to side, repeating in his tireless, marcato voice, 'Listen, Otraveskov, listen to me! I only want you to admit that I may be right, I only want you to say that Scheffler may have been a czar-paid man . . .'

Another interrogator appears, 'a dignified old gentleman, neatly dressed' and apparently reasonable. In due course, he presents the confession he wants; he wants it signed only 'as a formality'.

The trial of Scheffler, too, is only a formality. Yet Hutchinson's skill allows even the most monstrous of the characters enough humanity to make them credible. Mme Druvalov, wife of the secretary of the Political Department of the Judicial Committee, explains why Scheffler is on trial:

> With him, it is always the individual who matters. He cannot think of the millions who have suffered and who will go on suffering if we allow the acquisitive and cruel to have their way again . . . a new Russia is not to be made in a single generation – as we are making it – if every small step is to be clogged by petty scrupulosities.

Yet a moment later she says to her husband, 'Pyotr, you are not to go back to the court before you've had something to eat.'

The novel gives a vivid sense of the sheer chaotic muddle of the revolution, and its dislocating and destructive terror. For most people, to know what was happening anywhere except in one's own street – sometimes even in one's own street – was impossible. The vision in *Testament* is personal, from the ground up; there is no panorama, no sweep of history. Some of the scenes are almost cinematic set-pieces: the storming of a prison from which Scheffler is rescued, the charge of Cossack cavalry into a barricade, an auction in a palace where the Princess Roumaniev tries gaily and desperately to raise some cash by selling her belongings, including a painting almost certainly by Vermeer.

Perhaps most vivid of all are the disjointed final scenes when Otraveskov manages – with forged papers provided with the secret help of his revolutionary sister (who had once described her brother as 'an epitome of lukewarm intellectual benevolence without direction') – to escape from prison to join his wife and son on a boat fleeing the revolution. The passengers have to demolish a landing-stage to get wood for fuel, and a dozen horsemen follow the boat, firing their rifles from the bank while the boat breaks through the ice on its way to freedom.

Count Scheffler finds his own version of freedom. Just before his execution, he manages to smuggle out of the prison a letter to his friend.

> It's fixed for tomorrow now . . . I thought that all I had tried to do was wasted, I thought that every battle was lost and no voice left against the driving power of evil. And now I see that the seed you plant stays in the ground while the grass above it shrivels and burns, and the fire can't touch it, and the soil made up of old dead things will keep it alive and ready to give new life . . .

As Otraveskov stands at the front of the boat taking him and his wife and son away from Russia, it is this letter that he reads.

Goodness – in this case, heroic goodness, because Scheffler is offered a chance to leave Russia if he will sign a confession – is always harder to depict than wickedness or waywardness. In most of the novel, we see Scheffler very indirectly, even obliquely – he is in custody or in hospital, and the reader merely hears about him. Much of the impression we form is created by his wife, who is as much mystified by him as in love with him. Her realization that what she loves in him is precisely what makes him unable to compromise makes him credible to the reader.

This is not a comfortable or indeed a comforting novel. However, its range and passionate vivacity are such that one hopes its renewed availability will help restore Hutchinson to the pantheon of British novelists of the twentieth century.

C. J. DRIVER's early novels (*Elegy for a Revolutionary*, *Send War in Our Time*, *O Lord, Death of Fathers* and *A Messiah of the Last Days*) have recently been made available again as Faber Finds. There is more information about his most recent book, *So Far: Selected Poems 1960–2004*, at www.jontydriver.co.uk

The Great-aunt and the Author

CHRISTOPHER RUSH

I love finding things that have been stuffed long ago into old books – a letter perhaps, a photograph, or just an old laundry bill with its pounds and pence redolent of an older England, where once Chaucer rode to Canterbury and Falstaff drank his fill. Or more recently, where the Brontës conjured moonlit paths and Hardy drowned a mill.

The great-great-aunt Elspeth whose house we lived in during my 1940s Scottish childhood was a terrific reader of poems, many of which she recited to me from memory. In one forbidden drawer there was a quarto copy of Walter Scott's *Marmion*, which many years later I realized was a first edition. Among the other poetry books was the *Collected Poems* of Thomas Hardy, published by Macmillan in 1932. I didn't know it was there until the old lady died and my mother inherited a few of her possessions. It still sits on my shelves, in rather good condition.

And it still contains the items slipped between its pages by Elspeth. One of these is an original typescript of the poem 'Before Marching and After (In Memoriam F. W. G.)', dated September 1915, the month in which it was composed. It would be nice to suppose that it came from the Max Gate study and had been typed out on an old Remington by the slender fingers of Florence Emily Dugdale, Hardy's second wife and secretary. But a pencilled annotation in my great-great-aunt's hand reads: 'This was sent to me by Mr Herman

Thomas Hardy, *Far from the Madding Crowd* (1874)
Everyman · Hb · 480pp · £9.99 · ISBN 9781857150216

Lea after my visit to Thomas Hardy in July 1915.'

Lea, the much likelier typist, was a Dorset photographer and an intimate friend of Hardy – who shared very few intimacies with anyone, including his two wives. F. W. G. (Frank George) was a young relative of whom Hardy was sufficiently fond to be considering him as a potential heir, a possibility that was ended by Frank's death at Gallipoli in August.

That my Scottish great-great-aunt should have visited Thomas Hardy, getting through the combined defences of Florence Emily Dugdale and a ferocious terrier that helped keep visitors at bay, did not surprise me in the least. As a young woman in the 1890s she'd gone to Paris, got herself pregnant, and come back childless but with a nude painting of herself which still hangs in our house. So the intimation of a visit to the famous Mr Hardy by the formidable old lady struck me as just part of a life that was obscure but not without incident, not unlike the lives of many of Hardy's characters.

A second bookmark is a cutting from the *Daily Mail* of 26 April 1922, containing 'a new poem by Mr Hardy: News for Her Mother', which had just taken pride of place in the newly published *Dorset Year Book* of 1922, produced by the Society of Dorset Men in London. And a third is a single-column undated newspaper article covering a lecture on Thomas Hardy by Lord David Cecil to a local Scottish branch of the Association for the Speaking of Verse. In Oxford female students were wont to swoon at his lectures. The Scottish audience merely observed his hands, elegantly and expressively fingering the large manuscript volume of notes, to which however he rarely referred, speaking almost entirely from memory.

Cecil said that while Hardy could be called a romantic, expressing what he felt, deeply, personally, he did not conveniently fall into any category, and seemed to write almost for himself, following the impulse of the moment. This could easily have made him an introspective and egotistic writer, but the truth was that Hardy remained at heart a countryman. He was a very simple type.

The speaker went on to identify three strains in Hardy's writing: the lyrical, the dramatic and the philosophic. Hardy was a singer and a scripter, intensely alive to the bold storyline. He had the ballad strain in him, part of his upbringing. But behind lyric and drama and atmosphere lay his huge brooding view of life. His was a speculative mind, which argued from the particular to the general, forcing up from the depths of his meditations the questions that most concerned him, questions about man's position in the universe: why are we here? what conditions our lives? what are we striving for? what hope have we of getting it?

And the conclusion appears to be a sad and gloomy one. Man is the victim of forces which do not share his own moral feeling, hence the tragic irony of his life. At the same time Hardy conveys in his work an extreme sense of the sheer pleasure of life – not at all a gloomy affair, if the affair happens to go your way.

Whether my great-great-aunt attended that meeting, I shall never know. She died in 1947 and the meeting took place well before then. But those who did listen that evening were privileged to hear a simple, succinct and penetrating analysis of Hardy, the like of which our contemporary literary criticism, lost in its wasteland of jargon and academic abstraction, simply can't provide.

In one of her journal entries Elspeth draws the distinction between chastity and virginity, with reference to Mr Hardy's Tess. In another she writes simply: '*Far from the Madding Crowd*, his favourite, and mine'.

His favourite. Did Hardy ever say so? Not to my knowledge. And if there ever were a stated preference, I doubt whether it was made public until long after she penned this note. My delightful conclusion finds Elspeth sitting with the great man in 1915 and asking him which of his own books he liked best. I wonder what he thought of her. He was 75 at the time. She was 45 – and very striking.

I read Hardy's novels in my late teens without knowing much about the author. And my own position hasn't changed in 50 years.

With *The Return of the Native* running a close second, it is still *Far from the Madding Crowd* that offers the most satisfying read. A country boy with a fossilized village upbringing and a close affinity with the natural world, I was naturally drawn to Hardy, and to this story in particular with its deliberately evocative title. And I imagined the book would be a literary extension of my own rural habitat.

'Timeless Tranquillity': by Howard Phipps

We lived out between the sea and the fields – where horse-gear still jingled and the farmers still laid out the harvest as they had done for centuries in house-high haystacks. Hardy's rustics were people I knew personally. In my adolescence I conducted the customary love-affair with language and literature. I mooned around country churchyards, pretending I was – not Thomas Hardy, but Thomas Gray. I loved his *Elegy*, written for the dead of Stoke Poges, and I had it by heart. Roaming the curving beaches and broad acres of the East Neuk of Fife, I spouted the poem aloud to an audience of seagulls and sheep, enjoying the moment when I stood among my own village tombstones and spoke the famous stanza:

Far from the madding crowd's ignoble strife,
Their sober wishes never learned to stray;
Along the cool sequestered vale of life
They kept the noiseless tenor of their way.

Little did I realize that in Stinsford, close to Hardy's birthplace, Hardy had done exactly the same, and when his secretary once remarked to him that Stinsford was 'a Gray's Elegy sort of place', Hardy answered: 'Stinsford *is* Stoke Poges.' Gray's Stoke Poges, Hardy's Stinsford, my own St Monans, they all embodied the obscure and timeless tranquillity I imagined awaited me in the novel.

In fact it's not a pastoral idyll at all. Sheep don't safely graze, storm and fire wreak havoc, and in one grotesque scene a demonic gargoyle spouts holy rainwater from on high, to churn a newly planted grave into a mush of mud and upturned bulbs, making a mockery of Christian burial.

And in his troubled landscape Hardy places people whose lives are equally troubled. Three men chase the same woman. One is driven mad and murders another; one abandons another woman to a wretched workhouse death. The third, virtuous man gets the girl and the gold in the end, but by then three people have died, four lives have been wrecked, and you are left with an alarming understanding of just how fragile is our apparent integration with our environment.

I recall closing the book thinking: well, if this is far from the madding crowd, give me daffodils! Later on of course I realized I'd been reading Hardy at his most refreshingly idyllic. The book is a picnic compared to the novels that follow, and there's a spaciousness about it that is invigorating and elemental. It's a cliché of Hardy criticism that his novels are like Greek dramas, bible stories, old ballads, Shakespearean plays, and the story of Bathsheba Everdene and her three lovers has something of all these in it. But ultimately it's a classic example of the accuracy of the Lord David Cecil critique, as delivered to that Scottish audience. Hardy's deepening pessimism was to lead to a kind of literary imbalance, but in *Far from the Madding Crowd* he is still singer, scripter and sage par excellence. He is still what Cecil calls him – a simple type.

The novel was originally called *The Poor Man and the Lady*, echoing Hardy's own social frustrations, but by adding not only a soldier (Francis Troy) and a gentleman farmer (William Boldwood) but also an abandoned woman (Fanny Robin) as the unscrupulous soldier's sweetheart, Hardy transcends the simple ballad with a rich narrative that is beautifully balanced and integrated and that keeps you on the edge of suspense. It's easy to imagine Victorian readers running down to the newsagent's first thing in the morning to pick up the next serial instalment.

But you don't fall in love with a book on account of its symmetry. The characters have to engage you, and they do me. Infatuation, flirtation, sincerity, self-seeking, obsession – they ring the changes on human love. Boldwood's descent from dignified bachelor untouchability to blind compulsion bordering on madness is a story that is upsetting and unforgettable. It speaks to me in a Shakespearean way about the seeds of self-destruction contained within us all.

Most of us manage to maintain our equilibrium in this world. Gabriel Oak does and Francis Troy doesn't, as their names may imply. The Boldwoods of the world must beware the Bathshebas, as again the ironic echoes of the names suggest. Bathsheba is a biblical image of temptation. Eve, Everdene, evergreen – a beautiful woman may make you happy forever, but her merest whim can smash your world to pieces. Fate is fickle – and female.

Ultimately I must be an optimist – I like the Virtue Rewarded plot. The poor man wins both lady and land, returning the story to its simple classic level, and at the end of this book I experience the 'feel good' factor, as if I've just eaten a full English breakfast. Everything's on the plate.

And it wouldn't have worked without the rustics. They are the pastoral equivalent of Shakespeare's artisans, the rude mechanicals of *A Midsummer Night's Dream*. As such they are not just rustic stooges, there for local colour, choral comment or comic relief, but the backbone of the older England Hardy loved, a personification of a country that has all but disappeared. There is no better portrayal in our literature of the harmony that used to exist in our old communities.

They are also an embodiment of the natural world itself, which informs this particular novel so intimately that the setting becomes a character in the plot, perhaps its chief character. Quite simply it fills me with a sense of spiritual healthiness. Bad things do happen in nature, but nature has its own way of sorting them out. In the end, Hardy gives me hope.

Elspeth died when I was 3. She'd met Hardy, who was born in 1840, and who in turn knew older people who belonged essentially to the eighteenth century. The landscape he depicts in *Far from the Madding Crowd* is the pre-industrial landscape of his forebears. His novel tells me that quite simply time is a trick played on us. We are told that life is short – and it is. But at times it also seems long, especially when people of vastly different ages interconnect. I'm standing with one foot solidly in the third millennium . . . and there's another ghostly footprint somewhere in the eighteenth century. When you bridge time like that, through people and books and scribbled notes, you do feel, even momentarily, that you are indeed far from the madding crowd.

CHRISTOPHER RUSH has been writing for over 30 years. His books include *To Travel Hopefully* and *Hellfire and Herring*, and *Will*, a novel about Shakespeare. He is currently working on a novel about Odysseus.

End of a Baltic Summer

RICHARD KNOTT

'That is the only church built in Russia during the Soviet era,' the guide said, pointing at a bleak white building near the shoreline. A few more yards and we could see the full sweep of the Baltic from one promontory of Tallinn Bay to the other. The water had a steely look to it. This was the venue for the sailing events in the Moscow Olympics in 1980, and the grudging attempt at church-building was meant for those athletes who valued prayer. The skyline was a profile of what history has done to this Estonian city: blocks of soulless high-rise flats from the Stalinist era, a clutch of small-scale skyscrapers and docked cruise liners dwarfing the old part of the city.

I had taken the coach from Riga to Tallinn. The landscape was flat; spruce and pine trees; sheets of water; storks ponderously struggling into flight. The border with Latvia was open, policed only by flocks of house martins in the eaves of the border crossing's roof. I dozed, catching up on the sleep I had missed the night before when I had been reading till two in the morning. Then I had been sailing into the Bay of Tallinn in a 30-foot ketch, tacking into the wind, heading towards 'the three ships of the Estonian Grand Fleet and the rock and spires of Reval, dim in the rain'. There had been a crew of three – four including me – and the year was 1922. The yacht's captain was Arthur Ransome; Reval was the old Germanic name for Tallinn; and the book was *Racundra's First Cruise* (1923).

I had bought my Travellers' Library blue hardback copy for 40

Arthur Ransome, *Racundra's First Cruise* (1923)
John Wiley · Hb · 240pp · £20 · ISBN 9781898660965

pence years ago; my diary tells me I read it for the first time in February 1984. In those days I slept better, but there was compensation lying awake in Riga in the early hours with Ransome at the tiller, the 'Ancient Mariner' – 'a very little man, with a white beard and a head as bald as my own' – and the 'Cook' whom Ransome, without a glimmer of guilt, believed 'was the one who worked her passage'. The male sailors had to be fed after all.

Arthur Ransome and I both liked Tallinn, though he would not have recognized what progress has done to it. Strange to think that the Russian Orthodox church, with its onion-domed extravagance, was just two decades old when Ransome, walking through the cobbled streets, past wooden buildings with horsehair in the mortar, under a fortified gateway and up a long slope within the inner wall, was confronted by what he thought of as 'the fantastic Russian church'. He would have shaken his head at the crocodiles of tourists marched through the old city by relentless guides holding flags aloft, and the swarms of pesky sellers of postcards in the main square.

I liked the terracotta roofs, the shadows cast by trees, the way buildings nestled into each other, the climb up through the old town. I liked the great sweep of the bay too, the unexpected blue of the Baltic which I had imagined grey and wind-whipped. Ransome warmed to the city well enough, but it was the sea that held him. At one point in the book he declares: 'I cannot believe that any man who has looked out to sea from Reval castle rock can ever be wholly happy unless he has a boat.'

There is little about politics in *Racundra*. Ransome is more concerned with wind and tide than he is with Estonia's struggle to free itself from the Russian bear. These days, in the Baltic, the struggle for independence is still a recent, raw memory. The culminating event in that struggle in Estonia was the Singing Revolution. Imagine that – 300,000 Estonians gathered together and singing, voices reaching out to defy, then defeat, the occupation. Later, on 23 December 1989, almost 2 million Estonians, Latvians and Lithuanians stood, hand in hand, on the Baltic Way, stretching from Tallinn to Vilnius – 400 miles of protest.

Ransome opens a narrow but perfectly shaped window on a world that was rapidly disappearing in the years after the Great War, and now seems like ancient history. From the moment you look at the map with which the book opens, with its dotted lines marking the path of the plucky *Racundra*, and its obscure islands through which the ketch must navigate to make for Reval and Helsingfors, you know that what matters here is the journey – the compass, barometer, canvas and tiller; prevailing winds and anchorages.

The plucky *Racundra*

The voyage takes place as the summer is fading away, and the reader is frequently reminded that a Baltic autumn is just over the horizon. The boat-builder Ransome had commissioned to build *Racundra* had missed a series of deadlines through the summer and it was 20 August before the boat was in a fit state to sail. *Racundra* was designed to be a cruising boat in which 'a man might live from year's end to year's end'. She made her new owner inordinately proud: 'Master and Owner of the *Racundra*. Does any man need a prouder title or description? In moments of humiliation, those are the words that I shall whisper to myself for comfort. I ask for no others on my grave.'

Ransome, his crew and new boat sailed from Riga in Latvia, bound for Helsingfors (now Helsinki). The plan was to test out *Racundra*'s seaworthiness as well as to explore some of the more remote Baltic islands. Soon after setting out, we approach the first lonely island with Ransome: Runö, 50 miles out from Riga, where 'its Swedish seal hunters [are] using words that in Sweden have become archaic, living . . . a life of medieval communism'. Sliding tentatively through narrow sea passages, in shallow water, you can almost hear the scrape of the boat's hull on submerged rocks. There are fogs and dead calms when time seems to stand still; anxious navigation that comes out right in the end; and days of uplifting and exultant sailing when all seems right with the world. 'It was a glorious day, bright hard sunshine, with cold in the air, as we get in the Baltic at the back end of the year, a good wind heeling her over to the railing, stiff as she is, and that mighty swell lifting us sky-high and dropping us again into a blue depth walled by water.' I am there with him, me under a single sheet on a steamy night in Riga, and Ransome and his motley crew, bounding across the Baltic on a day made in heaven.

Ransome wrote *Racundra's First Cruise* seven years before the publication of *Swallows and Amazons*, the first of the children's stories he would write over the ensuing 17 years (see *SF* no. 18). Previously he had been caught up in the tumult of the Russian Revolution, as a journalist with the *Daily News* and increasingly as a confidant of the Bolshevik regime. His second wife Evgenia (whom he married in 1924 in the British Consulate in Reval) had been Trotsky's secretary. Writing about *Racundra* proved intensely liberating for him. This is a book which gives us a clear insight into where its writer's future lies, seven long years before Ransome first sent John, Susan, Titty and Roger across the lake in *Swallow*, bound for Wild Cat Island.

The sea, the crew and the resilient *Racundra* are the chief characters in the book, and they have an endearing charm. We also encounter some memorable people along the way, invariably in a crisp prose that has an ozone quality to it. There is the time when *Racundra* anchors off Ermuiste, 'which means "the terrible", for it is a place of many wrecks'. (Ransome leaves you in no doubt that the Baltic is not for the faint-hearted: storms appear in an instant; ships sink.) Here, amid the tumbledown ruins of a disused harbour, he finds 'the great golden body of an unfinished ship'. An old man with a face of 'clear walnut' is building the ship and has been so doing since the harbour was abandoned, many years before. It is a loneliness that daunts the visiting writer, who leaves the place wondering what the old man's future holds: will he ever sail in the ship he has spent a lifetime building?

Perhaps the most haunting section of the book is the meeting between Ransome and Captain Konga, skipper aboard the *Toledo*, once of Leith. She is stuck fast on a shoal – a particularly problematic issue in the tideless Baltic – and Konga has been sent by the Salvage Company to oversee her recovery. It is proving a long job. He is living on board in a makeshift cabin scarcely bigger than himself. In splendid isolation, in a winter-frozen sea and through hot continental summers, he fishes, makes nets and thinks of his lady friend in Hull whom he has not seen for twenty-five years.

Captain Konga is at the mercy of the sea – he cannot remain marooned forever, and his fate chimes with the fact that *Racundra's First Cruise* was written when a great wave was about to engulf a way of life. This is a story where the reader is privileged to stand beside a writer in tight control of sails and prose; where for a brief moment we can share in something that would soon disappear forever. At the book's end, with papers in order and 'nothing to declare, formalities . . . quickly over, the ensign hauled down', *Racundra* is laid up for the winter. You step ashore, legs still shaky from those days at sea, smelling oil and salt in the air and listening to the tinny sound of halyards thrashing masts, and step back into the modern world, where oversized cruise ships tie up nose-to-tail at Tallinn's dockside. Still, there is a kind of solace in the slim hardback in the traveller's pocket, with its tales of the Baltic long ago.

RICHARD KNOTT has sailed infrequently and usually with cabin-boy status.

Drama in Dulcimer Street

SARAH CROWDEN

Somewhere in our loft, there is a box containing jigsaws, board games and a very particular pack of 'Old Maid' cards dating from the 1940s. This game is played by making up pairs of cards, finally leaving one player holding the 'Old Maid'.

The pairs in this pack show types of the time, drawn in quasi-cartoon style – a jolly postman, benign doctor, snooty butler, nursemaid, pilot, land girl, and so on. They last saw the light of day in 2011, during rehearsals for Trevor Nunn's production of Terence Rattigan's 1941 play *Flare Path* at the Theatre Royal Haymarket in which I appeared as Mrs Oakes – 'the hotelier from hell', as she was described in the *Daily Mail* review.

Although the Landlady is not one of the types represented among the playing cards, she was a familiar figure of the time. Her forbidding exterior usually revealed a heart of gold, as it does with Mrs Oakes, whose gruff Yorkshire demeanour serves to hide her emotions as she cares for the pilots of Bomber Command in a hotel in the Lincolnshire Wolds.

The cards caused interest and hilarity during rehearsals, and, as further research, I also looked out a fondly remembered novel, *London Belongs to Me* by Norman Collins, which is set in a Kennington boarding-house. It begins in 1938, at Christmas, with the threat of war looming, and covers a two-year time-frame, ending at Christmas 1940, only a few months after the first London Blitz. It

Norman Collins, *London Belongs to Me* (1945)
Penguin · Pb · 752pp · £10.99 · ISBN 9780141442334

was fascinating to read it again surrounded by the 1940s props and costumes for *Flare Path*. As the story unfolded, it began to feel contemporary, rather than the quaint period piece it had seemed the first time I read it. The narrative voice reminded me of the soundtrack of a Pathé newsreel, imparting information in a manner both chummy and confiding.

London Belongs to Me is Norman Collins's best-known book, first published in 1945, regularly reprinted throughout the fifties and sixties, once in 1977 and most recently by Penguin in 2008. The hardback edition I own is a 1949 copy, and runs to over 700 pages of small type. In 1948 it was made into a film with a cast of iconic British character actors, among them Alastair Sim, Joyce Carey, Fay Compton and Richard Attenborough. There was also a six-part television series in 1977, again with a roster of the best of British, including a young Trevor Eve.

A prolific novelist from the 1930s until the late 1950s, Norman Collins also had an extraordinarily successful parallel career. After a spell in publishing (he was Deputy Chairman of Victor Gollancz for seven years), he joined the BBC. As Controller of the Light Programme (1946–7), he was instrumental in setting up *Woman's Hour*. He then moved into television and, as Controller of the BBC, oversaw the transmission of the 1948 Olympic Games. He went on to become a founder member of ATV, now absorbed into the ITV network. His last novel was published in 1981, and he died a year later.

As a writer he has been compared to Dickens in the breadth and scope of his characterization, as well as for the geography of his setting, and indeed Dickens would have recognized much of Collins's London, and many of the people in it. Mrs Vizzard, the landlady of No. 10 Dulcimer Street, SE11, could be regarded as the novel's central character, though it is darling old Mr Josser – the man on the tram rather than the Clapham omnibus, who cries when he retires from his job as a lowly but loyal clerk in the City – who provides the book's continuity. Mr Josser is London's Everyman. He cares deeply about his fellow residents. His formidable wife, rarely referred to by her Christian name, is a tartar for propriety (though under her starchy exterior there beats a generous heart). Mr Josser, however, is largely untroubled by social convention. While Mrs Josser guards her family and their status at No. 10 like a fierce but loyal terrier, Mr J. is the conduit through which introductions to the other characters are made, and a series of 'if only's' set in train.

Nine people live cheek by jowl at 10 Dulcimer Street. The once lovely building, standing in a street of Georgian residences south of the river, is 'three storeys above and one below'. On the top floor lives Mr Puddy, a widower who, like most of the tenants and the house itself, has 'known better days'. Food and its accumulation are his *raison d'être*. 'Third floor back' is the chancer Connie, an elderly ex-actress who takes advantage of Mr Josser's kindly nature on a regular basis. On the next floor down are the Boons, mother and son, then the Jossers and their daughter Doris on the ground floor. Mrs Vizzard lives in the basement's 'nether depths', next to the soon-to-be-occupied back basement room.

The most unconventional resident of all arrives in response to Mrs Vizzard's newspaper advertisement, to take that empty room. One of literature's memorable charlatans, his poverty acute, his powers questionable, Henry Squales, aka Enrico Qualito the medium, is an actor's gift. He was played in the film, unsurprisingly, by Alastair Sim. For much of the novel, Squales is the answer to a widowed maiden's prayer, but ultimately his actions seal his fate when he exploits Mrs Vizzard's vulnerability and provokes her to revenge.

At the novel's heart is a murder, perpetrated by garage mechanic and small-time crook Percy Boon, and the consequences of this desperate act for the residents of No. 10. Like an anxious, affectionate relative, Collins returns time and again to characters not featured for a while to check on their welfare, so we always remember who and where they are and what they have been up to – something modern authors tend to forget. This epic, enchanting novel sprawls like the great metropolis it depicts and covers much ground. Here is a magical evocation of London life during an extraordinary period, which encompasses engagements, a serious illness, numerous changes of address, two weddings, the murder and the subsequent trial, the Blitz both from a distance and close up, and several deaths.

By the closing chapters, love in its many forms has triumphed, of course. Despite an uncertain future in a time of war, the Jossers end the book back in the ground-floor rooms of 10 Dulcimer Street, SE11, determined to sit it out where they belong, in Mr Josser's beloved London. Though their lives have been inexorably changed by the often tragic events they have experienced over the two previous years, the Jossers remain as devoted to each other as ever, content with their lot and comforted by routine and familiarity. As for the other residents, Collins skilfully ties up the myriad loose ends and apportions an entirely appropriate fate to each one.

It would be unfair to give away more of the plot. Suffice to say, this is a marvellous book and well worth investigating. A new TV adaptation is long overdue, and I'd very much like to be in it. Alas, now too old and the wrong sex to be cast as Percy Boon, and far too young for the ancient Connie, the solution for me must surely be to add yet another Landlady to my extensive CV, and play Mrs Vizzard.

SARAH CROWDEN reviews books for *The Lady*. The vagaries of freelance life have not, as yet, forced her to take in lodgers.

Right Reverend

RICHARD PLATT

George MacDonald is a man who changes lives. The friend who first handed me MacDonald's *Annals of a Quiet Neighbourhood*, the fictional memoir of the Reverend Henry Walton, Vicar of Marshmallows, discovered it decades ago, in its delicious three-volume 1867 first edition (ah, for those halcyon days!) when he was a graduate student in Germany. His newly-wed wife was also a graduate student who had recently given birth to their first child. Their financial resources were perilously strained and, as neither of them had read Erasmus on the merits of books versus food, were deemed insufficient for three-volume, leather-bound novels, however enchanting. There was nothing for it but to sit on the floor of the bookshop and read the book there. When he turned the final page several weeks later, he rose stiffly to his feet, went home, and announced his intention to become a minister. MacDonald had shown him the allure of devotion.

George MacDonald was born in rural, pre-industrial Scotland in 1824, into circumstances which today would be judged grinding poverty but which MacDonald later remembered with delight. He became a Congregationalist Minister after university but soon found himself without a congregation, his unorthodox, radical views being regarded as almost blasphemous. Unlike most of his Calvinist brethren, he chose not to preach of God's wrath and eternal Hellfire,

George MacDonald, *Annals of a Quiet Neighbourhood* (1867), is out of print. However, *George MacDonald: An Anthology*, edited by C. S. Lewis (1947) is available in paperback (Zondervan · 224pp · £8.99 · ISBN 9780060653194).

but of His infinite love and the mercy of divine grace. It was a vision difficult to sell to parishioners living in a bleak and forbidding climate, and in a world before the pain-killing blessings of chloroform. Unable to support himself and his growing family in the pulpit, MacDonald knew he still had something to say, and he turned to writing.

MacDonald published fifty-three books: sermons, novels, poetry, literary criticism and fairy-tales for children, and, as one would expect from such a prodigious output, his work is uneven. Some of his novels are heavy with Scottish dialect as thick as porridge, which is beautiful when read aloud, but can be hard work for readers without an ear for this lovely music. *Annals of a Quiet Neighbourhood* is a fine introduction to MacDonald for it is one of his most philosophically accessible as well as most readable books. Because the novel is heavily autobiographical, we meet MacDonald as a writer, as a thinker, and as a man. To spend time with him is to grow in mental health.

Since this is the first-person reminiscence of an elderly vicar, we may expect, and either welcome or skip over, a little sermonizing, but what in lesser writers would be insipid platitudes, in MacDonald are eternal verities. They are so deeply and honestly felt, so *audible*, and so joyously offered, that they cannot help but resonate in an open heart and mind. Like the finest teachers, he never pushes. He leads. His tone is gentle, and while his belief rests on a foundation of bedrock he is never self-righteous. He hates what is hateful, but is ashamed to glimpse in his own heart a contempt for those who act hatefully. A becoming and heartfelt humility is ever present. He welcomes intelligent and thoughtful inquiry, believing that the legitimate end of argument is not victory but Truth, and that the ability and willingness of the agnostic to express doubt is actually a duty. It is a hallmark not of intellectual weakness or spiritual blindness, but of honesty.

MacDonald's vision of goodness encompasses not merely what is good in man, but what is good in everything around him. At his best, his ability to conjure rural beauty is not unworthy of Thomas Hardy.

> The slanting yellow sunlight [on a great bed of white water-
> lilies] shone through the water down to the very roots anchored
> in the soil, and the water swathed their stems with coolness and
> freshness, and a universal sense, I doubt not, of watery presence
> and nurture. And there on their lovely heads, as they lay on the
> pillow of the water, shone the life-giving light of the summer
> sun, filling all the spaces between their outspread petals of liv-
> ing silver with its sea of radiance, and making them gleam with
> the whiteness that was born of them and the sun.

MacDonald lifts the commonplace into the realm of the sacra-
mental. When the Reverend Walton arrives in his new parish,
friendless and wet, on a dreary, dark, rainy winter day, he is feeling
sorry for himself. He has been greeted only by a row of pollards, a
form of tree he particularly dislikes but in which he ultimately rec-
ognizes the virtues of strength and resilience:

Mary Kuper

> Pollards always made me miserable. In the
> first place, they look ill-used; in the next
> place, they look tame; in the third place,
> they look very ugly. I had not learned
> then to honour them on the ground that
> they yield not a jot to the adversity of their cir-
> cumstances; that, if they must be pollards,
> they still will be trees; and what they may not
> do with grace, they will yet do with bounty;
> that, in short, their life bursts forth, despite
> all that is done to repress and destroy their
> individuality. When you have once learned to honour anything,
> love is not very far off.

Walton is a man easily contented. He is content with a soft breeze
at his study window, a comfortable chair to read in, a good book

bound in vellum or full calf (even he is not immune to this most laudable form of covetousness), and good work to do. Our fallen nature being what it is, there is plenty of good work for him to do. His is the world of Victorian Melodrama: assignations on Dark and Stormy Nights, an Ageing and Once-Grand Manor House, scene of Dark Deeds, witness to Shameful Secrets, complete with Hidden Passages, a Mysterious Pool, a Scholarly Recluse, a Proud, Imperious Mistress, and a Beautiful Daughter, her large dark eyes 'burning as if the lamp of life had broken and the oil was blazing', betrothed to a Scoundrel she does not love, for of course she is in love with Our Hero, the vicar. Just beyond the confines of The Hall, we have the Fallen Woman, the Self-Important Church Warden, the Star-Crossed Young Lovers, and the Common Villagers, none of whom is common in MacDonald's hands. It is Walton's mission to mend what is broken, foster what will grow, nurse what will heal, and pray for what will die. He will, mostly, succeed.

Walton moves through his parish with the compelling confidence of utter belief, tempered with a genuine simplicity, a dread of becoming a 'moral policeman', and a humility that is born not of personal inadequacy but of a deep understanding of his place as servant and disciple, which shields him from the slightest taint of sanctimony. His humility is the conscious choice of a thinking man, awake, alert and alive, his mind in first-class fighting trim. It is not his place to judge – except when he judges himself – only to serve. In serving the daily needs of his parish there are victories and defeats, and the inevitable friction of a small community where the vicar is forced occasionally, though unwillingly, to take sides. But Walton is so quick to forgive that his forgiveness almost precedes his rebuke, softening it into a gift: an offer of wise counsel.

One of his parishioners, the local carpenter Thomas Weir, has suffered a crushing, life-changing disappointment: his only daughter has given birth to a child out of wedlock. Consequently, Weir has lost his faith in God's benevolence, and has turned his jaundiced eye on the deficiencies he suddenly sees in the world around him. The Reverend Walton, who knows that a man might have a better reason for staying away from church than a vicar has for going, allows the hostility that arises from this good man's sorrow to have its head and expend itself. Weir, himself a master craftsman, expresses the quite understandable opinion that if God did create the world, he has made rather a bad job of it. This prompts Walton, who has been watching him work, to suggest that the coffin he is making is perhaps not Weir's best work either. Taken aback, and a little offended, Weir reminds the vicar that the coffin is unfinished, and that his work should be judged not by what it is now, but by what it will be, and what it is for. The comparison with their world becomes obvious. Their conversation ends in a respectful détente. When the tale is told, they will be friends.

Not every parishioner in Marshmallows is in need of the young vicar's ministrations, as he soon learns. Having broken the ice with the village's hard-nosed sceptic, Walton seeks out Old Rogers, the retired seaman who had been the first to welcome him to the parish, his face a study in 'roughness without hardness', and 'endurance rather than resistance'. Walton soon sees that this 'simple' man has been placed in his path not to be instructed by him but to teach him, to show him what his own Christian faith actually looks like when it walks and breathes. Rogers, his heart uneasy, confesses that whenever he has a moral question to decide, he asks himself what *He* would do in the same situation, and if he can see his way clear to that, that's what he does, no matter what anyone says. He wonders if perhaps he is too stubborn and obstinate. Walton, chastened, and a little ashamed that he had presumed to instruct a better man than himself, says simply, 'Stick with that.'

Because he has such a firm grasp of goodness, MacDonald is supremely sure-handed in its representation. One need only recall Oscar Wilde's quip about the death of Little Nell to realize how seldom even the greatest writers have been able to create a convincing portrait of goodness: a portrait that is whole and deep and powerful rather than spiritually priggish or insipid. As C. S. Lewis, who regarded MacDonald as his master, pointed out in his *Preface to Paradise Lost*, no writer can create a better man than himself, as no stream can rise higher than its source. The depiction of evil requires him to be less than he is. The depiction of goodness requires all of the man, usually more than he is. To create evil characters, one need only release the brake of conscience or societal taboo, and the demons rush forth. But to create a better man than himself, a writer has to rise like a winged creature. He has not the resources.

It is easy to believe that MacDonald was a man without enemies, as all those who left an account of him attest. He is the most unapologetic of apologists, yet his goodwill is as infectious as laughter. You may disagree with him, but tread lightly. MacDonald grasped goodness as Newton grasped mathematics. He may be wrong, but he sees further up and further in than most of us, and with immense clarity. For a time, his fame, and his fees for speaking engagements, could rival even that of Charles Dickens; his ability to draw crowds of thousands to hear him lecture on William Blake is surely a testament to the miraculous. It took the weary cynicism of the First World War to destroy his popularity. MacDonald lived to see the birth of the twentieth century, but fortunately, not its ugliness. We are the poorer for his good fortune. The twentieth century could have used a bit more goodness.

RICHARD PLATT would like to be a better man than he is. George MacDonald is helping him.

Lion-hunting with the Colonel

STEPHEN HONEY

I expect that most of us, particularly in the current economic climate, have experienced trying times in our working lives, whether dealing with uncooperative colleagues, rude customers or overbearing management. However, next time you feel inclined to grumble, spare a thought for Lieutenant-Colonel J. H. Patterson, the author of *The Man-eaters of Tsavo*. His account of the extreme difficulties he endured while employed as an engineer on the construction of the Uganda Railway at the end of the nineteenth century is a sure way of keeping one's own problems in perspective – all the more so since Patterson bore it all without a hint of complaint.

In 1898 John Henry Patterson was commissioned to oversee the construction of a section of the railway that would link the port of Mombasa with Nairobi, running through a large expanse of hostile terrain in the Tsavo region of what is now Kenya. Upon arriving at the construction site in March of that year, he found that his workforce was beset by a number of problems. In addition to friction between the Hindus and Muslims in the camp, his employees included several 'scoundrels and shirkers' as well as stone masons who 'had not the faintest notion of stone cutting'.

In order to establish his authority and keep the building work on schedule he had to resort to

John Henry Patterson, *The Man-eaters of Tsavo* (1907)
Wilder Publications · Pb · 152pp · £5.99 · ISBN 9781604597455

unorthodox methods. So when one particularly recalcitrant individual, Karim Bux, took to his sickbed claiming to be at death's door, Patterson decided to persuade him to return to work by piling

Daniel Macklin

some wood shavings under his bed and setting them alight.

To ensure that the masons did a fair day's work, he introduced a piecework system of payment by results, and this caused a number of them to start plotting against him. One day, during an inspection of the quarry, he was surrounded by a large group of angry men carrying crowbars and flourishing heavy hammers. As they closed in, 'one burly brute, afraid to be first to deal a blow', hurled the man next to him at Patterson – 'If he had succeeded in knocking me down, I am certain I should never have got up again alive.' However, the seemingly unflappable engineer stepped aside and, taking advantage of the confusion, sprang on to a rock and successfully faced down the murderous mob by haranguing them in Hindustani.

As if this weren't enough, shortly after Patterson's arrival two large lions began to stalk the workers' camp by night, dragging their victims from their tents and carrying them off into the bush before devouring them. After a Sikh worker named Ungan Singh was taken, Patterson set about tracking the lions' path, eventually finding an area covered with blood, strips of flesh and bones, with Singh's head lying a short distance away, 'the eyes staring wide open with a startled, horrified look in them'.

Despite the erection of high thorn barriers and the nightly lighting of campfires, these attacks continued for nine more months and began to exert such a strong hold over the minds of the labourers that they believed the lions to be the spirits of two tribal chiefs angered by the encroachment of the railway. At one stage the attacks became so frequent that the workers downed tools and fled, bringing construction to a complete standstill.

Clearly something had to be done and the resourceful Patterson (who had served in the army in India and was an experienced tiger-hunter) set about hunting down the lions using a variety of methods. These included improvising a trap out of wooden sleepers, tram rails and some lengths of wire and chain, and spending the night camped out on top of a raised platform. There is palpable tension in his account of sitting out night after night, listening to the sound of the lions stalking the brush below. With typical understatement he writes, 'If one of the rather flimsy poles should break, or if the lion should spring the twelve feet which separated me from the ground . . . the thought was scarcely a pleasant one.'

After several fruitless attempts, Patterson's determination eventually paid off and by the end of the year he had shot both lions. They turned out to be massive specimens, measuring over nine and a half feet from nose to tail. By the time they were dispatched, they had devoured no less than twenty-eight of his Indian workers as well as 'scores of unfortunate African natives of whom no official record was kept'.

Patterson's account of his lion-hunting is very matter-of-fact: indeed he comes across as the epitome of the phlegmatic British colonial. However, as well as earning him the respect and admiration of his formerly mutinous workers (who presented him with a silver bowl inscribed with a message of thanks), his exploits were mentioned in the House of Lords by the Prime Minister, Lord Salisbury, and have formed the basis of at least three films, most recently *The Ghost and the Darkness*, released in 1996.

While he had little choice but to hunt down the man-eaters in order to protect his workers and continue the railway's construction, Patterson was also an enthusiastic big-game hunter and managed to dispatch a staggering array of creatures, including eight more lions (the photographed heads of which form the book's frontispiece), two warthogs, a leopard, a zebra, a rhinoceros, two snakes and a hippopotamus (which he describes as being 'without doubt the ugliest and most forbidding looking brute I have ever beheld').

Yet he declined an opportunity to shoot a giraffe on the grounds that 'it is a pity to shoot these rather rare and harmless creatures'. And, while we might find his passion for big-game hunting hard to understand today, he did at least recognize the need to preserve the range of species he encountered and was pleased that the country south of the railway, up to the boundary of German East Africa between the Tsavo River and the Kedong Valley, had been designated as a game reserve.

The Man-eaters of Tsavo, first published in 1907, is an engaging book on a number of levels. First and foremost it is a gripping tale of adventure. However, its author also has a keen eye for geography and provides a fascinating portrait of the area then known as British East Africa, before the railway opened it up to colonial settlement and enabled the export of coffee and tea. It is illustrated with a selection of Patterson's own photographs, featuring everything from the two man-eaters after they had been shot (propped up in lifelike poses) to the indigenous peoples he encountered.

As to the final fate of the lions, after a speaking engagement at the Field Museum of Natural History in Chicago in 1924, Patterson agreed to sell their skins and skulls to the museum for the then sizeable sum of $5,000. The animals, which had previously been displayed as trophy rugs in Patterson's house, were reconstructed and put on permanent public view, where they can still be seen today.

STEPHEN HONEY has worked in publishing for over 20 years during which time he has been called upon to perform a variety of tasks. He is grateful that these have yet to include hunting man-eating lions or facing down a murderous mob.

Finding Gold

MARTIN SORRELL

Those 150 pages were very timely, I now remember, because in just a few escapist hours they cleared my head of the months of swotting for university finals. The weekend before my exams started, a friend who'd left the college sent me a small package containing a paperback which he'd inscribed with a line from Wordsworth, 'Up up my friend and quit your books', and his own suggestion that I take his gift and a bottle into a field somewhere, and indulge myself in a sunlit afternoon of plain pleasure. Two weeks later, exams over, lying not in a field but on a sofa, I opened the book without great expectations, but from the gripping first chapter I was hooked. I read it through in one go. With or without a bottle, I can't say, but definitely it would have been with cigarettes.

The book in question was *Moving Target* (1966), a man-on-the-run thriller by a New Zealander called Jack McClenaghan. After I left university, I forgot about the book. Then, last year, decades later, sorting out drawers, I happened upon an empty packet of Gold Flake. A faint aroma of Virginia tobacco lingered still. The sight and smell of that neat packet transported me in a trice back to the summer of *Moving Target*. In my mind's eye, I suddenly saw its cover, title, author's name and a wintry scene in which a packet of Gold Flake featured prominently. Now I wanted that book again, to hold it, to reread it. Inevitably, my copy had vanished. And it was out of print. So I resorted to the Internet.

Jack McClenaghan, *Moving Target* (1966), is out of print.

Days later, there it was in my hands, *Moving Target*, in the Panther Crime series. My memory hadn't played tricks. I'd forgotten the words splashed above the title, assuring me I wouldn't read a more exciting novel that year. I'd forgotten too the blurb on the back which told me that this was the best manhunt since *Rogue Male*. But the cover illustration was indeed a wintry scene, a snowfield on which were scattered a few objects evocative of toughness and just a little tenderness – a pocket compass, a metal whistle stamped with the maker's name (Adie Bros., Birmingham, 1941), a mountaineer's piton, a clip of five brass-tipped bullets, a black-and-white photo of a pretty woman whose blouse failed to hide much of her left breast, and a packet of Gold Flake cigarettes, lid open.

Jack McClenaghan was born in 1929, but whether he's still alive I haven't been able to ascertain. I can only hope he is. He's published at least two further novels and a couple of geographical guides. At the time of *Moving Target* he was a journalist based in Invercargill, the most southerly city in New Zealand, where he was assistant editor of the *Southland Daily News* and made a bit of a name for himself as a feature writer with a particular knowledge of Fiordland, New Zealand's largest national park. In web searches, *Moving Target* is the title that pops up most frequently. It tends to get mentioned in the same breath as *Rogue Male* – that yardstick again – Geoffrey Household's 1939 classic of the manhunt genre (see *SF* no. 22).

Moving Target is set at the very south-west tip of New Zealand's South Island, in rough country clearly modelled on Fiordland. The action takes place during the Second World War in a range of mountains called the Yeleas, sixty miles long and between eight and fifteen miles wide, wild terrain much better suited to animals than humans. (As I haven't found them on any map, I have to assume the mountains are fictitious.) Despite the harshness of the landscape, gold prospectors have sought their fortunes in its rivers and some are still working their concessions when war breaks out. The New Zealand government has served call-up papers on a young bushman and prospector called Jim Dougherty. In his own good time, Dougherty reports for training. But he and the army don't mix. It's not that he's weak or cowardly – far from it – or that he doesn't like human company. Nor is he a conscientious objector or pro-German. He's no thinker; he's not in any way political, unlike the hero of *Rogue Male*. It's simply that army life is incomprehensible to him and he wants none of it.

After a few uncooperative months, Dougherty walks out and heads back into the Yeleas. If nations want to squabble with one another, that's their affair. It's not his business. He lives life differently, by instinct and reflex. What he resembles is an intelligent animal superbly adapted to its environment. He's outside human morality; he's a loner whose affiliation is to nature. During his short time in the army, he behaves like a cat that can't be herded. Taken miles from its home, it turns around and finds the way back.

The army, however, has to herd its cats in order to function. Strays are not permissible. A search party under the leadership of Sergeant Campion is sent out to bring Dougherty in. Which is where the story begins. Dougherty the animal and Campion the tracker are well-matched adversaries. But while Campion's five senses are sharp enough, they're nothing like Dougherty's and, besides, Dougherty seems blessed with a sixth. He's in a different league altogether, and even the other mountain men know it well.

As soon as I'd finished *Moving Target*, with its surprising end which I won't reveal, I wanted to go straight to *Rogue Male*. I'd read Household's story once, as a teenager, but couldn't remember much about it except that an English aristocrat ends up trapped below ground somewhere in the West Country but contrives an ingenious escape. I got hold of a copy easily enough and found that Household's story gallops along just as quickly as McClenaghan's. I enjoyed it hugely, but on this second reading it seemed a mad fantasy. I half-expected the last page to reveal that the hero has just woken from a nightmare, not in a filthy subterranean hideout in

Dorset but in his club in St James, with only thirty minutes for breakfast and a visit from the barber before reporting to his Control. *Moving Target*, on the other hand, is a story with its feet firmly on the ground, a tale of the perfectly possible, economically told in clean prose. Well before its last, powerful page, I'd become fully engaged with that untamed mountain creature called Jim Dougherty, tough and rough maybe, but as human and vulnerable underneath as the rest of us.

If ever I find myself banished to a desert island, or a mountain cabin, I'd like to have *Moving Target* with me. It's my favourite thriller. And to be honest, I wouldn't mind a packet or two of Gold Flake

MARTIN SORRELL continues to read, teach and write about literature of all kinds, still without cigarettes.

How Alice Grew Up

JEREMY NOEL-TOD

Nicholson Baker's fifth novel, *The Everlasting Story of Nory*, was not, as its 9-year-old heroine might say, the world's most raging success. I picked it up as a pocket hardback in a clearance sale. A week later, I returned and bought the remaining stock at a pound apiece, to distribute to friends and family.

The book itself explains why I did this. In Chapter 39, 'Reading Tintin to Her Babies', Eleanor 'Nory' Winslow ponders the difficulties of communicating a literary enthusiasm:

> Sometimes the problem with telling someone about a book was that the description you could make of it could just as easily be a description of a boring book. There's no proof that you can give a person that it's a really good book, unless they read it. But how are you going to convince them that they should read it unless they have a glint of what's so great about it by reading a little of it?

Thankfully, magazines now exist that are dedicated to overcoming this problem. Rereading my last remaining copy of *Nory* for this piece, however, I wished I had gone to the wholesalers and taken a boxful, because there are few books that ask so much for the proof of being given.

For me, *The Everlasting Story of Nory* is a profound exploration of the origins of civilization through the mind of a child. But that

---

Nicholson Baker, *The Everlasting Story of Nory* (1998), is out of print.

could, admittedly, be somebody else's idea of a boring book. And so could this, from the dust-jacket:

> A nine-year-old American girl . . . is spending a term at an English school. She thinks about teeth, tells herself stories, defends a classmate, has nightmares about cows, and generally does her best to make sense of life's particulars as she encounters them.

Like the boys in Nory's class who emit 'low gurgles and snickers' when she has to read her story about a girl who makes friends with a dog, not to mention the English teacher who bans the word 'nice' (even though it is 'a very, very important word for kids'), the book's reviewers were not impressed. 'A thin, highly predictable narrative about a schoolgirl's banal – and uneventful – life' (*New York Times*); 'a dull book' (*Guardian*); 'readers who are not relatives will wish [Baker] had edited and focused the book more stringently' (*Daily Telegraph*).

This last faintest praise alludes to the story behind the book's dedication: 'To my dear daughter Alice, the informant'. Spending a family year abroad in the cathedral town of Ely, the American Baker would collect his daughter from school every day, 'interview' her about her experiences, and work them up into fiction. Which sounds, of course, like the most tender self-indulgence. The impulse to share, as a parent, is irresistible, but the endless story of little Johnny is best kept for a select audience.

Baker's account of Nory's development in an interview seems artless: 'I didn't know how the book would end up because I didn't know how her experience in this English school would end up.' But the artfulness of the book begins, in miniature, with the title. Like a number of the novel's epithets, 'everlasting' turns out to be more accurate than its conventional synonym ('never-ending'). This is not a fairy-tale of eternal childhood. Growing up is at the heart of Nory's story, which ends with a loose tooth and 'a salty taste of blood in her mouth'. Yet her narrative is concerned with the 'everlasting' in that it depicts the deep continuities between child and adult mind, including the irrepressible desire 'to be continued', as Nory says at the end of her own stories. The word 'everlasting', she notes, recalls 'the kind of things you say in Cathedral', which is also the place where she learns about the never-ending story she knows, by a slip of the ear, as the 'crucifiction'.

Baker's critics tended to regard the book more as a sort of Everlasting Gobstopper, the endlessly sweet sweet invented by Willy Wonka in Roald Dahl's *Charlie and the Chocolate Factory*. The novel's gentle blending of third-person narration with Nory's own thoughts resulted in a 'veneer of cutesiness' that made it 'almost unreadable'. Never judge a book by its veneer, though. As in Dahl, only more so, the salty taste of the uncute cuts constantly through Baker's storytime style, with an irony too subtle for actual children.

Mary Kuper

The conceit of a book about a little girl who tells herself stories 'the grown-up way, the way she loved to talk' inevitably recalls the great Daisy Ashford, and her *Young Visiters* (see *SF* no.28). And Daisy and Nory are, indeed, of an age. But where Ashford wrote in precocious imitation of adult romances, Nory's unfinished epics are fantasies of self-reflection. 'The Story of the Deadly Rain', for example, follows its 'eight or nine years old' heroine, Mariana, on one of her regular trips to the Sahara Desert. She soon finds herself having to rescue another little girl, 'about the age of four', from an unexplained onslaught of boiling raindrops. 'Her face started bubbling it was so hot. Her sweat turned red with blood . . . Mariana spoke softly to the girl. "Do not cry dear, do not cry, it takes blood from your precious body".'

These are the true melodramatic imaginings of childhood, prompted by the previous chapter's waking experience of school fire drill and drama class ('they were learning to die in various ways'). Through stories, Nory finds a way of transforming her small, unconnected observations into grand, meaningful chains. To quote Henry James, the ventriloquist of another naïvely perceptive little girl in *What Maisie Knew*, 'art *makes* life, makes interest, makes importance . . . and I know of no substitute whatsoever for the force and beauty of its process'.

There is no substitute for art in *Nory* because it is everywhere. The little girl who wants to be a dentist or a pop-up-book maker, who has a plan to curate 'a museum of fake food from all different lands', and who uses stories to avoid bad dreams and to deepen friendships, is an instinctive improver of the world. I hesitate to say that she embodies Baker's theory of fiction, because that makes her sound like the heroine of a boring book again. But there is undoubtedly a nod towards this in the self-portrait of Nory's father, whose contribution to the world is 'writing books that help people go to sleep'.

Nory is a bedside book in the best sense: it comforts and amuses, and translates the world with dream-like lucidity. Another of the book's fortuitous malapropisms is Nory's friend who reads 'totally emerged in the page'. Like Alice entering Wonderland, immersion in a story becomes emergence in another world. When Nory has a nightmare that recalls Alice's fall down the rabbit hole – she becomes a white rabbit who burrows into an ancient corpse in the cathedral grounds – she wakes up, reads a book and regains imaginative control:

> Ah, yes, she saw her mistake . . . the dead monk was not really dead – it was just sleeping deeply, wearing a frightening mask . . . the black tongue was made of papier-mâché and had a little spring that made it pop out.

It is Nory's interest in the workings of everything, cute or disgusting, that makes her an artist in waiting. She is equally fascinated by the idea of a doll's egg with rubber insides that will 'goosh out' when cracked and the blood that would 'coosh out' from a pig's bladder used by an Elizabethan actor. (Her scene-stealing younger brother, 'Littleguy', whose head is filled with the technical vocabulary of trains – a doughnut with icing is 'mixed-traffic' – also shows promise.) By adopting this naturally attentive view of the world, Baker writes about his year in England in a way that corrects all the abstraction of adult life, for which the book has little time ('Nory's father had to go in to London . . . to look something up').

Every other page in my copy has a pencil-marked moment of pleasure. My favourite chapter follows Nory's thoughts in Ely Cathedral's Lady Chapel, its skeletal windows and walls 'broken up very tiresomely' by the Reformation and Civil War. Performing her own restoration, she arrives at one of the book's many associations of art with the care of parenting:

> Right now the Lady Chapel definitely had problems, in Nory's opinion. It smelled very coldly of stone. Probably that was because the stone powder was always falling, since there were so many places that the stone was broken open, and over the years it kept falling from them, like pollen . . . Long ago it would have been a much, much more Mary-Mother-of-Goddish sort of building when the stained glass was there, because the colours would be red and blue and you might feel you were in a humongous stone kangaroo pouch.

> I hope that gives you a glint.

JEREMY NOEL-TOD teaches English Literature at the University of East Anglia in Norwich. Occasionally, he has to go in to Cambridge to look something up.

Such Devoted Sisters

JAMES ROOSE-EVANS

Edith Olivier, born in 1872, was one of ten children whose father was for nearly fifty years Rector of Wilton, on the estate of the Earls of Pembroke, outside Salisbury. After the death of their parents, Edith and her beloved sister Mildred were invited by the Earl of Pembroke to live, at a peppercorn rent, in the old Dairy House (which Edith renamed as the Daye House) in Wilton Park. When, in 1924, Mildred died of cancer, Edith was desolate. She wrote in her journal, 'I cannot realize that I am going to be lonely always.' Being a devout Anglican – each day of her life she went to an early Eucharist – she considered entering a convent, but at 52 she was told by the Mother Superior not only that she was too old but also that she was 'too rebellious of mind'.

The following year changed everything for Edith. She was invited by her neighbour, 19-year-old Stephen Tennant, the beautiful son of Lord Glenconner, to join him and a fellow student from the Slade School of Art on holiday in Italy, and it was then that she met the brilliant young artist Rex Whistler. He was to become like a much-loved son to Edith, and would illustrate eleven of the books she was to write.

Soon a whole galaxy of writers, artists and musicians began to gather at the Daye House for meals, weekends or even longer visits, including Siegfried Sassoon – who fell passionately in love with

---

Edith Olivier's *The Love Child* (1927) and *Without Knowing Mr Walkley* (1938), like the rest of her books, are out of print, as is Penelope Middelboe's *Edith Olivier from Her Journals, 1924–1948* (1989).

Stephen Tennant – William Walton, Harold Acton, Brian Howard, Lord David Cecil, Oliver Messel, the Sitwells and Cecil Beaton, who eventually leased his first home nearby at Ashcombe. And, of course, Rex. As Beaton wrote later:

> Of the neighbours on whom I grew to rely more and more, Edith Olivier was perhaps the most cherished. It was she who, by bringing me into contact with so many new friends, was largely responsible for my having blossomed into a happy adult life; and it was she who continued, without effort on her part, to discover young people of promise and bring them into her house. So many of the young writers, painters and poets came to her with problems about their life and work.

Edith was liberated by these young people. In her journal she describes Cecil Beaton arriving one weekend in his two-seater car with Rex Whistler, Oliver Messel and piles of luggage and furniture. 'I climbed in on to anyone's knees and we hurtled along through blinding rain and cruel wind, skidding round corners. Cecil approaches all corners at sixty miles an hour and then jams on the brakes! They are like schoolboys, rushing after each other, and fighting and shouting till all hours of the night!'

Edith Olivier in the 1930s, reproduced courtesy of Hugh Cecil, © Lord David Cecil album

Then, one evening, about eighteen months after the death of her sister, unable to sleep, she began to write what was to be her first and perhaps most memorable book, *The Love Child*. Long after it was published and she had written several more, she was asked why she had not written anything earlier. She replied that since childhood she and her sister had been the closest of companions: 'We often used to make up stories to entertain one another. We would tell each other that one day we would write books, but we found each other's companionship so completely satisfying that we sought no wider public.'

On 10 February 1927 she recorded in her journal: 'A great day! Got a letter from the publisher Martin Secker accepting *The Love Child* and saying he read it "with very great pleasure" and will publish it at once. He only received it on Saturday and wrote this letter on Tuesday. I simply can't believe it.'

The novel, born out of a sudden and intense imaginative energy, opens with its central character, Agatha Bodenham, left on the death of her mother in solitary occupation of a large house. She recalls how, as a child, she had created an imaginary companion called Clarissa with whom she had shared everything. But when she was 14 her governess, finding out about Clarissa, had put a stop to such make-believe games. Yet Clarissa had meant more to Agatha than any real person so that, in losing her, she had also lost part of herself. Now however, in her loneliness, she begins to talk to the imaginary Clarissa, who eventually becomes visible to Agatha, though to no one else.

More and more Clarissa inhabits Agatha's life as the two become totally dependent on one another. Suddenly, however, Clarissa becomes visible to other people and Agatha is forced to account for her by saying that she is a child whom she has decided to adopt. But then reality breaks in when the local policeman calls with a form requiring Agatha to state Clarissa's full name, parentage and date of birth. If she fails to do this, the child will be taken from her. Quite unprepared, Agatha finds herself saying from somewhere deep inside her, 'She is a love child. She is my own.' This, psychologically, is the truth, but no sooner has she said it than she realizes everyone will now look on Clarissa as her illegitimate child.

By now Clarissa is 17 and has made friends with the Rector's daughter, Kitty, who introduces Clarissa to her cousin David. He falls in love with Clarissa, and Agatha, like Phaedra, is consumed by jealousy. The way in which Edith Olivier handles the tragic climax of her story is both brilliant and haunting. At the moment Clarissa vanishes, Agatha cries out to David, 'She was mine, mine only! I gave her life to her and you have taken it away!' As Lord David Cecil wrote in his introduction to a Virago reissue, 'It is Miss Olivier's triumph that the balance between fantasy and reality never wavers for an instant.' The book is, above all, a study of loneliness, and the power of psychological projection, for it is not only children who create imaginary companions.

Edith wrote many books, though none became a best-seller and she was always hard up. Where she most comes into her own is when she writes out of herself, as in *The Love Child* and in her autobiography *Without Knowing Mr Walkley*, published by Faber in 1938, which focuses on the places and people among whom she spent her life. The latter contains a memorable passage describing the occasion when Salisbury Cathedral was flooded:

> All through the night the water had been silently coming up through the floor, and by morning the nave was a large still pool, from which the pillars rose and into which they threw their reflections. The water did not reach the choir and services were held there throughout the flood, the congregation reaching them upon perilous bridges made of planks.

For sixty years Edith kept a journal, part of which, covering the period from 1924 to her death in 1948, has been edited by her great-great-niece Penelope Middelboe. It is a wonderful record, written with a total lack of inhibition and full of rare insights into the characters of Siegfried Sassoon, Ottoline Morrell and others. On a visit to Renishaw to stay with the Sitwells she writes:

> There is this feeling of mystery and madness. They say the house is haunted, but the ghosts are the living people. Every evening Lord Berners and Willy Walton play violent impromptu duets

on the piano in order to drive Sir George Sitwell to bed. When they succeed, we sit round and Osbert tells many amusing and cruel stories about Lady Colefax and the other people he dislikes.

With the outbreak of war Edith was put in charge of housing the evacuees who flooded into the area. Then, in July 1944, she learned that her beloved Rex had been killed in France. In her journal she wrote, 'To try to speak makes me cry. O Rex, Rex! . . . Everyone seems to know what he and I are to each other.' She was 72. She died four years later. As Cecil Beaton wrote, 'There was honour, indeed, for what she had done, but there was love for what she was and is. We were there because we loved her. We owe her so much.'

As Edith's coffin was lowered into the grave, a pigeon flew straight up into the sky with a great swish of wings. Cecil Beaton and David Herbert both gasped and said simultaneously, 'Edith soaring through tracks unknown!' – a phrase she herself had often used when speaking of death.

JAMES ROOSE-EVANS is a theatre director, and founder of the Hampstead Theatre. His most recent books include a memoir, *Opening Doors and Windows*, and *Finding Silence: 52 Meditations for Daily Living*. He has just adapted for the stage Philippe Besson's novella *En L'Absence des Hommes*, newly translated by Carl Miller.

A new biography of Rex Whistler will be published this November: Hugh and Mirabel Cecil, *In Search of Rex Whistler* · Frances Lincoln · Hb · £40 · ISBN 9780711232846.

Taking a Hint

JUDY SPOURS

I already had something of a habit of collecting old home-making manuals – 1950s 'Pins and Needles' books with instructions for making a rag rug or knocking up a stylish telephone table for instance, or Constance Spry's *Flowers in House and Garden*; and I'm very attached to a 1930s DIY book on how to lay lino, not least for its demonstration photographs of a man in a home-knitted V-necked sweater who looks very like my father. Nevertheless, I'd managed to restrict my collection to just a few bookshelves until I was commissioned to write a book about Victorian and Edwardian eating and drinking.

In periodical and book form I found millions of words of advice for Victorians. Most of it was directed at women, particularly the thousands of young married newcomers to the burgeoning middle class. Their rise up the class ladder always carried with it the fear of a slip back down, so they were keen to equip themselves with the appropriate know-how to secure their position. Nothing was left to chance; everything from modest wifely behaviour to the proper ventilation of bedrooms was carefully described.

Dinner parties to which the Joneses and the husband's business associates were invited were of particular importance. Setting the right tone and the right taste with the right accoutrements was crucial. As I read through an exhausting number of handy and not-so-handy hints on how to cook, entertain and furnish the home (a good part of it delivered by 'members of the aristocracy' presumed to be in a position to know the correct manner in which to eat a guinea fowl or take a plum stone out of one's mouth), a fictitious young woman took up residence in my mind.

Recently married, she is setting up home, in 1870, in a new suburban house to the east of the City of London, where her husband works as a legal clerk. His is the world of business, and it has been made abundantly clear that hers is home and hearth. I think she's called Amelia, and she is sitting in her parlour wearing a fine gingham dress and an unpretentious lace cap, surrounded by the contents of a brown paper package. It's a sweet domestic scene, but she looks alternately flushed with excitement and as terrified as a Wilkie Collins heroine.

Amelia's package has come from the bookseller, and it contains a small cross-section of my own reading matter, including *The Dinner Question or How to Dine Well and Economically* by a pseudonymous Tabitha Tickletooth (1860). The maxi-mum number for a dinner party is eight or nine, Tabitha says, which will encourage general sociability rather than 'coteries'. She advises on the mix of guests: 'Avoid "bores" of every kind, the parliamentary, the literary, and scientific varieties above all; and do not, as many eccentric persons often do, congregate oddities together.' *Enquire within upon Everything* of 1865 leaves not a domestic moment to spare with its information about the exact time in the season to pick walnuts, how to make a plain pea soup, to remove freckles, protect dahlias from earwigs, dance the gallopade quadrille or polish enamelled leather.

Also in Amelia's package is the hugely influential *Hints on Household Taste* by Charles Eastlake, subtitled *Etiquette, social ethics and dinner-table observances. Including the drawing-room, the toilette, domestic duties, etc.*, first published in 1868 and reprinted numerous times throughout the rest of the century. Eastlake was passionate about good, unelaborate design, his strict views sharpened by what he considered the overblown decorative tat on display on British manufacturing stands at the 1851 Great Exhibition. Amelia's lip trembles as she learns that her pretty floral parlour wallpaper may not be in the best of taste: 'There is a growing impatience of paper-hangings which would beguile the unwary into a shadowy suspicion that the drawing-room walls are fitted up with trellis-work for training Brobdingnag convolvuli,' snorts Eastlake.

This really doesn't seem fair, because Amelia has already read *Etiquette, Social Ethics and Dinner-Table Observances* (1860), essays 'designed to show how much domestic happiness depends on a due regard to the little politenesses of life – how much real misery is occasioned by their neglect'. The instruction she had followed there was that 'A sensible woman will always seek to ornament her home . . . No wife acts wisely who permits her sitting-room to look dull in the eyes of him whom she ought especially to please . . .' She had, admittedly, been a little disturbed by its patronizing tone – for example, its nudge at her dinner-party bravado: 'If there is an *épergne*, it may be placed in the centre of the table, to hold salad; but we do not admire flowers being placed in the *épergne*, because we do not eat flowers.'

How can she keep up? Amelia so dearly wants to be included in that 'we', to gain a firmer foothold in the middle class through apparently effortless displays of good taste and good manners. But the *de-haut-en-bas* tone of many of the manuals, written by professionals or simply by those more socially experienced, is at once educational and threatening. Even the 'hint' of so many of the titles has an aggressive undertone. At least Isabella Beeton has kinder, more straightforward advice in her 1861 *Household Management*, listing and explaining the duties and responsibilities of the mistress of the house without condescension and providing reliable recipes and sensible domestic priorities. But even here there's room for confusion about flowers, since her recommendation is that the dinner-party table should never be without them.

This wealth of advice about everything from the design of the cutlery to the correct size of a table napkin, from the margin of floor around a Turkey carpet to the decoration of a cold dish of vegetables in aspic makes me feel I am there with Amelia in her new home as we prepare for the strict social demands of an evening's entertainment. These manuals reveal the determination of energetic young Victorians to learn and to improve themselves. Amelia and her friends become eager consumers; they follow the rules set around new social relationships; and they revel in the possibilities offered by the home technologies of an expanding industrialized world.

The contrasts of this pivotal time in the lives of Victorians, who now look forward to a scientific future but with one eye still on a rural past, are perfectly reflected in the combination of modernism and nostalgia found in these compelling publications. They offer an unparalleled insight into the preoccupations and anxieties of the age, a fly-on-the-wall view of the busy and pressured domestic lives of women in particular. For me they make irresistible reading – startling but nevertheless impressive, amusing but endearing for their energy and aspiration. In these millions of worthy words, every detail of ordinary Victorian lives is revealed. I can see the colours of the paintwork in a hallway, eavesdrop on dinner-party conversation, smell a roast shoulder of mutton with onion sauce, and feel the crispness of a starched damask tablecloth under my white-gloved hands.

JUDY SPOURS has worked variously as a book and magazine editor, as a journalist and author, and in higher education. Her eating and drinking book, *Cakes and Ale: The Golden Age of British Feasting*, is published by the National Archives.

93

Bibliography

Nicholson Baker, *The Everlasting Story of Nory*   80

Norman Collins, *London Belongs to Me*   62

John Colville, *The Fringes of Power: Downing Street Diaries, 1939–1955*   24

Jane Duncan [Elizabeth Jane Cameron], *My Friends the Miss Boyds*;
    My Friend Monica   30

Edmund Gosse, *Father and Son*   35

Thomas Hardy, *Far from the Madding Crowd*   50

R. C. Hutchinson, *The Unforgotten Prisoner; Testament; Recollection of
    a Journey; A Child Possessed; Rising*   44

C. S. Lewis (ed.), *George MacDonald: An Anthology*

Jack McClenaghan, *Moving Target*   76

George MacDonald, *Annals of a Quiet Neighbourhood*   66

Penelope Middelboe, *Edith Olivier from Her Journals*   85

Alan Moorehead, *A Late Education*   13

Edna O'Brien, *The Country Girls; Girl with Green Eyes; Girls in Their
    Married Bliss*   19

Edith Olivier, *The Love Child; Without Knowing Mr Walkley*   85

John Henry Patterson, *The Man-eaters of Tsavo*   72

Arthur Ransome, *Racundra's First Cruise*   57

Henry Williamson, *Tarka the Otter*   7

Coming attractions . . .

ROBERT MACFARLANE follows the drove roads

SUE GEE picks the darling buds

ANTHONY GARDNER salutes the *Sword of Honour*

DAISY HAY takes to the stage

JULIET GARDINER hears laughter in the next room

JOHN KEAY dives into *Hobson-Jobson*

YSENDA MAXTONE GRAHAM confronts her bookshelves

JEREMY LEWIS has an irregular adventure

Think before You Click

Please support independent bookshops

'In the past three years Amazon has generated sales of more
than £7.6 billion in the UK without attracting any
corporation tax on the profits from those sales'
The Guardian, 4 April 2012

Independent bookshops, including Slightly Foxed on
Gloucester Road, do pay corporation tax on profits from
sales. Last year our contribution was enough to buy
schoolchildren over 2,000 books. With your help we could
pay for a librarian too.

The Royal Society *of* Literature

14 September Seamus Heaney in conversation with Alasdair Macrae (Stirling University)

17 September Rose Tremain & Andrew O'Hagan: 'Much have I travelled' (Somerset House)

2 October Ahdaf Soueif, Roma Tearne & Caroline Moorehead: 'Making people care' (Chatham House)

22 October Michael Morpurgo: 'The spoils of war' (King's College London)

24 October Colin Thubron & Artemis Cooper: 'Patrick Leigh Fermor: a celebration' (RGS)

5 November Jackie Kay: 'The V. S. Pritchett Memorial Prize evening' (Somerset House)

26 November Richard Ford: 'The Hawthornden Anglo-American lecture' (LSE)

28 November Margaret Atwood discusses her life and work (Canada House)

For booking information on the above events visit www.rslit.org, call 0207 845 4676 or e-mail molly@rslit.org.